The Common Sense Gospel

Not By "Faith Alone"

The Common Sense Gospel

Not By "Faith Alone"

by George Burdick

Saltshaker Publishing, LLC

Copyright © 2020, George Burdick
All Rights Reserved
Paperback: ISBN 978-1-7348591-0-2
Hardback: ISBN 978-1-7348591-1-9
eBook: ISBN 978-1-7348591-2-6
Saltshaker Publishing, LLC

Cover illustration by Sharon Araujo

Unless otherwise indicated, Bible scriptures are quoted from the King James Version (KJV)

Scripture quotations marked NKJV: Scripture taken from the New King James Version®. Copyright © 1982 by Thomas Nelson. Used by permission. All rights reserved.

Scripture quotations marked ESV are from the Holy Bible, English Standard Version, copyright © 2001, 2007, 2011, 2016 by Crossway Bibles, a division of Good News Publishers. Used by permission. All rights reserved.

Quotations designated (NET) are from the NET Bible® copyright ©1996-2006 by Biblical Studies Press, L.L.C. All rights reserved. Scripture and/or notes quoted by permission.

Scripture quotations marked (NLT) are taken from the Holy Bible, New Living Translation, copyright © 1996, 2004, 2007. Used by permission of Tyndale House Publishers Inc., Carol Stream, Illinois 60188. All rights reserved.

Billy Graham quoted from a campaign sermon in Washington, DC.

~ Table of Contents ~

PART ONE: The Basics 1
   Salvation, Future and Present 1
   "My Thoughts Are Not You Thoughts" 4
   Repentance 4
   Mercy, Grace and Redemption 7
   Past, Present and Future 10
   Justification 11
   The Holy Spirit 12
   Sanctification 13
   Faith 17
   Loose Ends re: Ephesians 2:8-10 19
   Justification and "Saved" In Different Contexts 21
   Salvation: The Receipt of Eternal Life 23
   Works 25
   Creation Is Not Finished 39
   "You're a 'Works Salvationist'" 43

PART TWO: Eternal Security 45
   "Once Saved, Always Saved" 45
   Warnings 46
   Twisted Verses 53

PART THREE: Other Doctrines 63
   After Death, What Happens? 63
   When You Die 64
   "Absent From the Body" 65
   Resurrections 67
   In Paradise the Same Day? 70
   The Gospel of The Kingdom of God 72
   The End of Evil 76
   The Fates 79
   The New Earth and the New Heaven 81
   The Soul and Hell 85
   The Spirit: The "Breath of Life" 93
   The Meanings of "Hell" 96
   Born Again 110
   Lazarus and the Rich Man 116

PART FOUR: Prophecy for the End of This Age 123
   Why? 132

PART FIVE: The Gospel, By Grace 138

Part One: The Basics

Salvation, Future and Present

Salvation. "Saved." We have to ask, "Salvation from what?" or "Saved from what?" In the largest sense, if our life—our very existence—ends then we have lost everything; we have no more hope, no more opportunities, no more anything. It would be nice to be "saved" from that. In fact, if we had eternal life, we would have endless opportunities. Endless hope. Endless time and ways to love and be loved. And nothing would be lost. Ultimately, salvation is about receiving everlasting life instead of perishing:

> **For God so loved the world, that he gave his only begotten Son, that whosoever believeth in him should not perish, but have everlasting life (John 3:16)**

There is a huge side benefit to having the hope of salvation, the hope of eternal life. That hope gives meaning and purpose—salvation in a more immediate sense—to our present, mortal life. Now we have something to build for, to anticipate. We have reason. We have purpose. We have hope. There is meaning!

What we believe about life, about our future, has a profound effect on how we live our lives in the present. Many believe their life, their very existence, will be blown out "like a candle in the wind," in hopeless oblivion. Sadly, many today are wrangling against depression, seemingly entangled, snared, in a "first you suffer, then you die" paradigm. Some anesthetize themselves with life's mundane pursuits, with substitutes which never satisfy. Others resort to drugs and alcohol to ease the pain of a meaningless existence. We have an ongoing epidemic of drug abuse and suicide—because there is an epidemic of hopelessness. It is all very sad, and unnecessary.

Could there be anything *better* than having the hope of eternal life? Yes! The apostle Paul described something even better, which we can have right now in this mortal life:

And to know the love of Christ, which passeth knowledge, that ye might be filled with all the fulness of God (Ephesians 3:19)

Yes: every one of us can connect—personally—with the Supernatural: we can know Jesus. We can enter His love and abide in Him. This is true life. Without that connection, that relationship, that love we are incomplete; we are spiritually thirsty. To know Him and His love is to be "filled with all the fulness of God." This is "the water of life" Jesus spoke of:

I will give unto him that is athirst of the fountain of the water of life freely (Revelation 21:6)

The only way we can enter eternal life is by knowing Jesus and the Father, abiding in their love and grace. Jesus explained:

And this is the way to have eternal life—to know you, the only true God, and Jesus Christ, the one you sent to earth (John 17:3, NLT)

Part 1: The Basics

Jesus explained to the Samaritan woman at the well:

But whosoever drinketh of the water that I shall give him shall never thirst; but the water that I shall give him shall be in him a well of water springing up into everlasting life (John 4:14)

Let's be honest about God: even if you witnessed supernatural miracles from God directly in front of you, you could still have doubt, suspecting there might be a trick of some sort. But if we each had a miracle happen to us personally that would be much more convincing.

So, can we each find evidence God exists, with a miracle in our own lives, in our own experience? Jesus once called on Peter to step off the boat and walk on the water. Did Peter get the miracle by remaining on the boat? Of course not: he had to step off the boat. The same goes for us today. We must each step off our boat, out of our comfort zone, to experience a miracle in our lives.

The book you are reading was written to share how to step off your boat and bring God's love and His grace—and the hope of salvation—into your life. The benefits of a spiritually healthy life permeate into our physical health. Positive thinking and outlook go hand in hand with healthy living.

There is a lot of misinformation out there. An awful lot. And many—most, in fact—are being misled and deceived. I hate to see that. It would be irresponsible for me to say nothing, to do nothing. So, here's a book about it.

"My Thoughts Are Not Your Thoughts"

For my thoughts are not your thoughts, neither are your ways my ways, saith the LORD.

For as the heavens are higher than the earth, so are my ways higher than your ways, and my thoughts than your thoughts (Isaiah 55:8,9)

That's right. Our thoughts and deeds are not like God's, not even close. Our corruption, our sin, is offensive to God:

But your iniquities have separated between you and your God, and your sins have hid his face from you, that he will not hear (Isaiah 59:2)

God will not accept our sinning ways, not even for a moment. And certainly not for an eternity! If we are to entertain any thought of eternal life with God, something's got to change. *We* have got to change. We've got to shed our old ways and be re-clothed in holiness:

Follow peace with all men, and holiness, without which no man shall see the Lord (Hebrews 12:14)

Repentance

So, how do we get there from here? How do we come to the holiness that is acceptable to God? What does God tell us to do? While preaching to idol-worshippers in Athens, the apostle Paul told them what God commands us to do:

And the times of this ignorance God winked at; but now commandeth all men every where to repent (Acts 17:30)

Oh no. There's that nasty word again: "repent." Here it means change your mind about continuing in sin; change your mind about continuing in a life lived apart from God. Change your mind from living for the self, at the expense of others, to living in love for others as well as for God.

Repentance is a state of heart and mind: having your heart and mind set on forsaking sin, putting sin out of your life, seeking to do God's will, seeking to please God, no longer living apart from God. Throughout the entire Bible, that is what "repent" and "repentance" are usually referring to.

It seems to be remarkably obvious that if our sins separate us from God, then we should commit ourselves to turning from sin. It's common sense. But no, there are many preachers who say God's saving grace is received by "faith alone" which means just that: by faith alone, nothing else required, not even repentance. Just "trust," they say, and you will be "saved" the very instant you just trust. Seems too good to be true. In fact, it *is* too good to be true.

We have all sinned. We all need God's mercy. God's mercy is *promised* to us upon our repentance:

He that covereth his sins shall not prosper: but whoso confesseth and forsaketh them shall have mercy (Proverbs 28:13)

Yes, that's repentance. It begins with conceding or confessing you have sinned. This means you must first accept that it is God, not yourself, who decides what sin is.

Let's go back to the beginning for a moment. Adam and Eve chose to "eat" from "the tree of the knowledge of good and evil." In other words, they decided that they, instead of God, would "know" or decide what was good and what was evil. They presumed to take God's place and determine for themselves what was right and what was wrong. For *that* they were put out of the garden, and excluded from access to the "tree of life":

> **And the LORD God said, Behold, the man is become as one of us, to know good and evil: and now, lest he put forth his hand, and take also of the tree of life, and eat, and live for ever:**
>
> **Therefore the LORD God sent him forth from the garden of Eden, to till the ground from whence he was taken (Genesis 3:22,23)**

When we confess sin, we are reversing the Adam and Eve error. We are implicitly acknowledging God as the decider of good vs evil. And we are admitting we have crossed the line and done evil in God's sight.

Okay, back to repentance. Just confessing we have sinned is not enough:

> **. . . but whoso confesseth and forsaketh them shall have mercy (Proverbs 28:13)**

We can not forsake sin if we do not first recognize we *have* sin. But it is the "and forsakes them" part which makes the difference. A bank robber might admit, confess, that he robs banks. Maybe he'd even feel a bit bad about it. If he goes out to rob another bank the next time he wants more money, is that repentance? Of course not. Nothing in his thinking and behavior has changed.

Feeling bad and confessing are not enough. Repentance is a change of heart accompanied by commitment and resolution to change, to mend our thinking and behavior. Feeling sorry may be entirely appropriate, but it is *entirely ineffective* unless accompanied by change. Common sense: without change, nothing changes: things are no different than before.

God wants family. He wants sons and daughters dwelling with Him forever. Those sons and daughters are being created—right now—through Jesus. This requires that we change and grow up, spiritually . . . doing the things we should do, as well as not doing the things we should not do. Outside of repentance, we will not change. Without change, we will remain separated from God. We will not be part of His eternal family.

Mercy, Grace and Redemption

Mercy is promised if we'll repent: confess and forsake sin, turning from a life lived apart from God:

. . . but whoso confesseth and forsaketh them shall have mercy (Proverbs 28:13)

So, what is the mercy? It starts with this: our past sins will be blotted out:

Repent therefore and be converted, that your sins may be blotted out, so that times of refreshing may come from the presence of the Lord (Acts 3:19, NKJV)

Notice the order of events. First, repent: have a converted heart, willing and committed to confess and forsake sin, seeking to do God's will. Then our past sins will be blotted out. The sins that separated us from God will be erased. With those past sins erased, we are no longer separated from God. Now it will be possible for "times of refreshing" to come from "the presence of the Lord." Acts 3:19 is a great verse because it says so much. We'll return to it often.

I hope you noticed the statement "that your sins may be blotted out." That's right: our sins remain—*not blotted out*—unless and until we come to repentance! This is so important to understand: our sins were not blotted out the moment Jesus died on the cross. Many, especially in the "faith alone" crowd, will try to tell you all sins "past, present and future" were erased when Jesus died on the cross. It is simply not true. They do not understand what Jesus meant when He said "It is finished." They do not understand *what* was finished. I'll say much more about this shortly.

Along with the blotting out of our past sins we'll have redemption from the death penalty earned for those sins. The penalty or "wages" for sin is death: perishing in death:

For the wages of sin is death; but the gift of God is eternal life through Jesus Christ our Lord (Romans 6:23)

IF we'll come to repentance, our past sins will be blotted out and the death penalty already earned for those sins will be lifted:

Let the wicked forsake his way, and the unrighteous man his thoughts: and let him return unto the LORD, and he will have mercy upon him; and to our God, for he will abundantly pardon (Isaiah 55:7)

We'll be redeemed from the death penalty we had

earned. With His death Jesus made a ransom *available*: He made His death *available* as a payment. His death is now *available* to cover the death penalty we've each already earned. That's the work He finished on the cross. Thank you, Jesus!

Without the ransom payment He made available, we would all be hopelessly bound to perish for our sins, repentant or not. But now, thanks to Jesus, we can have that mercy, that coverage, that redemption—as promised—if we will obey and repent, coming to God on His terms, confessing and forsaking sin.

Here's Jesus, explaining His mission in Matthew 20:28:

Even as the Son of man came not to be ministered unto, but to minister, and to give his life a ransom for many (Matthew 20:28)

"Ransom" in that verse is from the Greek word λύτρον ("lutron"). It is a noun, not a verb. Jesus died for our sins, as stated in 1 Corinthians 15:3; Jesus made His death, His blood, available as a ransom—the noun—to cover our death penalty. We were not ransomed (the verb) when He died on the cross. He made a ransom payment (the noun) *available* when He died on the cross.

Now, with that ransom available for us, we can have that mercy, that coverage, that redemption—as promised— IF we'll obey and come to God on His terms, in repentance.

Outside of repentance, we do not receive mercy. Our sins remain, not blotted out. And we will perish, unredeemed, paying our death penalty ourselves. That's why Jesus warned (in Luke 13:5):

. . . except ye repent, ye shall all likewise perish

That's right: our sins were NOT "paid for, past present and future" the moment Jesus died on the cross. We'll pay for our sins ourselves unless we come to repentance! Jesus made a ransom—His death, His blood—*available* to cover our sins whenever we commit them: past, present or future.

Regrettably many have been taught that all sins, "past present and future," were "paid for" the moment Jesus died. They have been told a lie. Presuming that all sins, "past present and future," have been paid for they go on to conclude that sin can no longer be a salvation issue. "After all," they say, "all sins have been paid for, present and future." Nothing could be further from the truth.

As we've seen, our sins remain—not blotted out—until we come to repentance. And outside of repentance we will perish, paying our own death penalty. Yet the myths that all sins have been "paid for, past, present and future" and that sin is no longer a salvation issue persist. Those myths are core tenets of the "faith alone" and "free grace" theologies. More about this later.

Past, Present and Future

Question: So, when we first come to repentance are all our sins, past, present and future then forgiven? No. At any given point in time, we only have past sins on our record. In the present, no one possesses future sins (unless they are caught in some kind of science-fiction time warp, lol.) Our *past* sins will be "blotted out" if and when we come to repentance.

Here is Peter, commenting that a lukewarm believer has forgotten "he was purged from his old sins":

But he that lacketh these things is blind, and cannot see afar off, and hath forgotten that he was purged from his old sins (2 Peter 1:9)

The apostle Paul made a similar statement. Believers have "remission of sins that are past" (Romans 3:25).

Suppose your teenage son or daughter has recently received their driver's license, and gets ticketed and fined for speeding. They say they're very sorry, but they have no way to pay the fine. As parent you might offer to pay the fine for them. But if they continue to speed, just as before, would you continue to pay their fines? Of course not. True repentance goes beyond apologies and feeling sorry. Talk is cheap; change needs to happen.

While we are mortal we will sin. God knows that. God is looking for repentance—a heart and mind determined to forsake sin and live according to His will.

For all those things hath mine hand made, and all those things have been, saith the LORD: but to this man will I look, even to him that is poor and of a contrite spirit, and trembleth at my word (Isaiah 66:2)

Justification

We saw in Isaiah 59:1,2 that our sins separate us from God. But believers—those who have come to God, confessing and forsaking sin—have received mercy. Their past sins have been purged, blotted out. Those past sins can no longer separate the believer from God. The believer is no longer under condemnation, having been redeemed from the death penalty earned for past sins. No longer separated and no longer under condemnation, they enter *justification*, made right with God. They will remain reconciled as they continue to walk "in the light," abiding in Him in ongoing repentance.

The Holy Spirit

Now they can begin a new life, the "times of refreshing" in "the presence of the Lord" we saw in Acts 3:19:

> **Repent therefore and be converted, that your sins may be blotted out, so that times of refreshing may come from the presence of the Lord (Acts 3:19, NKJV)**

And how are they in "the presence of the Lord"? Through the gift of the holy spirit, given to those who obey and come to God in repentance:

> **And we are his witnesses of these things; and so is also the Holy Ghost, whom God hath given to them that obey him (Acts 5:32)**

> **Then Peter said unto them, Repent, and be baptized every one of you in the name of Jesus Christ for the remission of sins, and ye shall receive the gift of the Holy Ghost (Acts 2:38)**

Please note: the above passages do not say we receive the holy spirit because we have faith! Faith is not even mentioned! There is a reason for that. I'll explain shortly.

Part 1: The Basics

Sanctification

Jesus made a ransom available when He died on the cross. However, His work is not finished. He is at work right now. Through the holy spirit Jesus guides us and helps us overcome: overcome slavery to sin. Provided we follow Him, He will lead us into His righteousness. Jesus says:

As many as I love, I rebuke and chasten: be zealous therefore, and repent (Revelation 3:19)

Jesus says:

He that overcometh shall inherit all things; and I will be his God, and he shall be my son (Revelation 21:7)

Creation is not finished: sons and daughters for the Father's eternal family are being created, right now, through Jesus. He is the potter, we are the clay. A relationship with Him

. . . yieldeth the peaceable fruit of righteousness unto them which are exercised thereby (Hebrews 12:11)

This is how we are made ready to receive the gift of eternal life and to inherit the Kingdom of God. God will not have slaves to sin in His eternal family. God will not allow slaves to sin into His Kingdom. Paul wrote:

Know ye not that the unrighteous shall not inherit the kingdom of God? Be not deceived: neither fornicators, nor idolaters, nor adulterers, nor effeminate, nor abusers of themselves with mankind,

> Nor thieves, nor covetous, nor drunkards, nor revilers, nor extortioners, shall inherit the kingdom of God (1 Corinthians 6:9,10)

Paul urged the believers in Ephesus to pursue righteousness . . . to grow up, spiritually:

> That ye put off concerning the former conversation [life, lifestyle] the old man, which is corrupt according to the deceitful lusts;
>
> And be renewed in the spirit of your mind;
>
> And that ye put on the new man, which after God is created in righteousness and true holiness (Ephesians 4:20-24)

Paul compared the "old man" to the "new man," led by—and also bearing the fruits of—the spirit:

> Now the works of the flesh are manifest, which are these; Adultery, fornication, uncleanness, lasciviousness,
>
> Idolatry, witchcraft, hatred, variance, emulations, wrath, strife, seditions, heresies,
>
> Envyings, murders, drunkenness, revellings, and such like: of the which I tell you before, as I have also told you in time past, that they which do such things shall not inherit the kingdom of God.
>
> But the fruit of the Spirit is love, joy, peace, longsuffering, gentleness, goodness, faith,
>
> Meekness, temperance: against such there is no law (Galatians 5:19-23)

Some have been told the holy spirit *makes* or compels you to repent and change. That is error, making it God's fault—not your own—if you don't repent and change. Jesus does not compel or force anyone to change. Through the holy spirit He leads us; we must choose to follow. We must choose to be led:

> **For if ye live after the flesh, ye shall die: but if ye through the Spirit do mortify the deeds of the body, ye shall live.**
>
> **For as many as are led by the Spirit of God, they are the sons of God (Romans 8:13,14)**

Revelation 3:19, again, shows the interactive, synergistic nature of our relationship with Jesus:

> **As many as I love, I rebuke and chasten: be zealous therefore, and repent (Jesus, in Revelation 3:19)**

This choice to leave sin—and to be led out of sin, forsaking sin—is repentance. We are not called to repent once, then forget about it. No: we are called to active, ongoing repentance. Here is 2 Peter 3:9:

> **The Lord is not slack concerning his promise, as some men count slackness; but is long- suffering to us-ward, not willing that any should perish, but that all should come to repentance (2 Peter 3:9)**

In repentance we are clay in His hands. That is the only way Jesus can work with us. It is the only way He can lead us out of slavery to sin. It is the only way He can lead us into His righteousness. It is the only way we can be prepared to receive eternal life and inherit the Kingdom.

Otherwise, we remain outside His grace and mercy and will perish:

> **. . . except ye repent, ye shall all likewise perish (Luke 13:5)**

We can not make the journey along the "narrow way" (Matthew 7:14) that leads to eternal life without His help. And that journey can neither begin nor continue without our repentance, abiding in Him. He knows we need His help; He is ready to help us. Paul wrote:

> **I can do all things through Christ which strengtheneth me (Philippians 4:13)**

Of course, even after coming to repentance we will sin. We're not perfect: we're human. Paul wrote that if we get "out of line" God will reveal it to us:

> **Brethren, I count not myself to have apprehended: but this one thing I do, forgetting those things which are behind, and reaching forth unto those things which are before,**
>
> **I press toward the mark for the prize of the high calling of God in Christ Jesus.**
>
> **Let us therefore, as many as be perfect, be thus minded: and if in any thing ye be otherwise minded, God shall reveal even this unto you (Philippians 3:13-15)**

If we continue on with a repentant heart, walking "in the light," new sins will be blotted out as they occur. Jesus' blood remains available to cover us:

> **But if we walk in the light, as he is in the light, we have fellowship one with another, and the**

blood of Jesus Christ his Son cleanseth us from all sin (1 John 1:7)

Note that this cleansing is active, in the present tense: "cleanseth us"—not past tense. Once again, we see that our sins were neither blotted out nor paid for when Jesus died on the cross. *Our past sins are covered when we come to repentance; new sins are covered, cleansed, as we continue in repentance.* While we continue abiding in Him in repentance—walking "after the spirit"—we remain in justification:

There is therefore now no condemnation to them which are in Christ Jesus, who walk not after the flesh, but after the Spirit (Romans 8:1)

Faith

We've seen that God's mercy and grace are promised to those who come to repentance. So, what role does faith play? What is faith? Is faith necessary?

We can put two verses together and answer those questions. Let's start with Ephesians 2:8, a favorite "go to" verse among the proponents of "faith alone":

For by grace are ye saved through faith; and that not of yourselves: it is the gift of God

Yes: salvation comes by God's grace. Grace is received through faith. **Through** faith . . . not just because we **have** faith! Regrettably, many assume they'll receive saving grace if they just *have* faith, but that's not what the verse says. The verse says *through* faith. So, what does "through" mean? Let's turn to Hebrews 11:6 and continue:

But without faith it is impossible to please him:

for he that cometh to God must believe that he is, and that he is a rewarder of them that diligently seek him (Hebrews 11:6)

Faith is trust that God exists, and rewards. It would be impossible for a person to choose to "come to God" if he/she did not trust that God exists. And even if we trusted that God exists, we could not "come to God" without trust that there was some point or reward in doing so. But through faith—through trust that God exists and rewards—it becomes possible for us to decide to "come to God." Without that trust, that faith, it is impossible for us to "come to God."

Of course, it is that choice, that decision to "come to God" that matters . . . and pleases God. *With* faith we *could* choose to come to God. But that does not mean we *would* choose to come to God. There is such a thing as dead faith: we could still choose to remain in our old lives rather than come to God on His terms. We could choose to continue seeking the world's attractions and approval instead of God. That would be dead faith. Faith alone is dead.

What are God's terms? How do we "come to God"? We've been through that: God "now commands all men every where to repent" (Acts 17:30). If we'll obey, we'll receive His mercy as promised (Proverbs 28:13) and we will enter into His grace. In His grace, through His grace we will receive salvation: the promised gift of eternal life.

Faith "is the gift of God" (Ephesians 2:8), given to us to call us. Question is, will we answer the call? Will we "come to God" on His terms?

Part 1: The Basics

Loose ends re: Ephesians 2:8–10

Having said all that, there are a few loose ends that should be tied up. One loose end is the "works" mentioned in the verses immediately after Ephesians 2:8; another is the "by grace are ye saved" in Ephesians 2:8.

Here is Ephesians 2 verses 8 through 10:

8. For by grace are ye saved through faith; and that not of yourselves: it is the gift of God:

9. Not of works, lest any man should boast.

10. For we are his workmanship, created in Christ Jesus unto good works, which God hath before ordained that we should walk in them.

Paul wrote "For by grace are ye saved" in verse eight. Many immediately conclude, therefore, that they have been saved: past tense, done deal . . . if they just have faith.

But wait . . . hold on just a minute: we have other verses—also written to believers—saying we "shall be" saved. And other verses saying believers have "the hope of salvation" and are "appointed . . . to obtain salvation." Here's Paul:

But let us, who are of the day, be sober, putting on the breastplate of faith and love; and for an helmet, the hope of salvation.

For God hath not appointed us to wrath, but to obtain salvation by our Lord Jesus Christ (Paul, in 1 Thessalonians 5:8,9)

That's right: Paul did not tell them they *had been* saved. He said believers are "appointed . . . to obtain salvation." As you are probably well aware, that is quite a bit different from what is so often taught in churches today: you're already "saved" and have "eternal security."

The apostle Peter is consistent with Paul, teaching that believers, both "we" (Israelite) and "they" (Gentile), "shall be saved," in the future. Here's Peter addressing an assembly of apostles and elders:

> **But we believe that through the grace of the Lord Jesus Christ we shall be saved, even as they (Acts 15:11)**

So on one hand we have "For by grace are ye saved," apparently past tense (with a suggestion of *are being* saved, present tense) in Ephesians 2:8. But on the other hand we have "through the grace of the Lord Jesus Christ we shall be saved," future tense, in Acts 15:11. And we have "the hope of salvation" in 1 Thessalonians 5:8. What's going on? Is the Bible contradicting itself?

No: "saved" refers to different things in different contexts. So, what had the Ephesian believers been "saved" from? As believers they had been redeemed: saved from having to perish as the wages of their past sin. They had been saved from hopeless condemnation. They had received this mercy, as promised, because they through faith had chosen to come to God in repentance. Having entered into justification and grace—and remaining in justification and grace—they now had "the hope of salvation." They were now "appointed . . . to obtain salvation." They hoped to receive the promised gift of eternal life, by grace, at Jesus' return. That's the "shall be saved" that Peter was talking about in Acts 15:11. We'll read more about that shortly.

While we're here there is something I would like to point out. The passage from 1 Thessalonians 5:8,9 (quoted above) started with "But let us, who are of the day . . ." In 1 John 1:7, also quoted earlier, we have a similar opening:

But if we walk in the light, as he is in the light, we have fellowship one with another, and the blood of Jesus Christ his Son cleanseth us from all sin (1 John 1:7)

Being "of the day" and walking "in the light" both allude to the believer not hiding or covering sin, but rather walking in the light provided through the holy spirit: walking in ongoing repentance, confessing and forsaking sin.

Justification and "Saved" in Different Contexts

We have another verse saying believers "shall be saved." Here we see justification—in this present mortal life—clearly separated from salvation at a later time:

Much more then, being now justified by his blood, we shall be saved from wrath through him (Paul, in Romans 5:9)

"Being now justified . . . shall be saved." *Justification and salvation are different things, at different times!*

Paul was writing to believers. Through faith they had chosen to come to God, confessing and forsaking sin. For that they had received mercy and grace as promised: their past sins had been blotted out. They had been redeemed "by his blood." They would be saved—saved from ever perishing in death—in the future, when they received the promised gift of eternal life at Jesus' return. They had "the hope of salvation" as Paul wrote in 1 Thessalonians 5:8,9.

In the Ephesians 2:8 context they *had been* "saved"—past tense—from the death penalty they had earned for past sin. They *had been* saved from hopeless condemnation. Now, no longer separated from God by past sin and no longer under condemnation, they had entered justification.

In justification, they had entered "the presence of the Lord" (Acts 3:19) via the gift of the holy spirit. Note that Romans 5:9 does not say "having been justified"; their justification was not just a one-time, past-tense event. The verse says "being now justified": their justification was an ongoing, active standing as well as a past event. As they continued to "walk in the light" in repentance, any sins they committed would be covered by his blood (1 John 1:7). "Through him" (Romans 5:9) they would become "his workmanship" (Ephesians 2:10) and be made into the "new man" (Ephesians 4:24). They *were being* "saved"—present tense—from slavery to sin. They *were being* made fit to receive the gift of eternal life.

They *would be* saved—saved from ever perishing in death—in the future, when they received the gift of eternal life at Jesus' return. They had "the hope of salvation"—the receipt of eternal life—as Paul wrote in 1 Thessalonians 5.

Those who preach "faith alone" usually also say they have been "saved," past tense. They mean saved, "done deal," with "eternal security," meaning that the "salvation" they presume to have can not be lost.

Truth is, they may be in justification but they do not have eternal life. No one will be saved, "done deal," until they actually receive eternal life at Jesus' return. No one will have eternal security until they actually receive eternal life. Only then will "once saved, always saved" be true. Outside of receiving eternal life they will perish, totally unsaved.

Meanwhile in this mortal life any of us can enter into justification. And we can "fall away" from justification, no longer in His grace and no longer on the "narrow way" that leads to eternal life. How? By reverting to un-repentance, no longer abiding in Him. We have many warnings not to let that happen. We do need to be concerned about falling away from justification. If we do, we'll forfeit our hope of salvation. I'll have more about this later.

Salvation: the Receipt of Eternal Life

During this mortal life we may enter justification with God. As we remain in justification, we remain in His grace. And we have the promise of eternal life, to be received—by grace—at Jesus' "revelation" or return:

And this is the promise that he hath promised us, even eternal life (1 John 2:25)

Wherefore gird up the loins of your mind, be sober, and hope to the end for the grace that is to be brought unto you at the revelation of Jesus Christ (1 Peter 1:13)

In a letter to the Corinthians, Paul gave the following description of the receipt of immortality at Jesus' return. Jesus returns "at the last trump" (the seventh of seven figurative end-time trumpet soundings described in detail in Revelation chapters 8 through 11.) At Jesus' return the dead in Christ—"asleep" in their graves—will be resurrected "incorruptible": immortal. At the same time those in Christ who are alive at His return—not "asleep" in death—will also receive immortality:

> **Now this I say, brethren, that flesh and blood cannot inherit the kingdom of God; neither doth corruption inherit incorruption.**
>
> **Behold, I shew you a mystery; We shall not all sleep, but we shall all be changed,**
>
> **In a moment, in the twinkling of an eye, at the last trump: for the trumpet shall sound, and the dead shall be raised incorruptible, and we shall be changed.**
>
> **For this corruptible must put on incorruption, and this mortal must put on immortality.**
>
> **So when this corruptible shall have put on incorruption, and this mortal shall have put on immortality, then shall be brought to pass the saying that is written, Death is swallowed up in victory (1 Corinthians 15:50-54).**

Here is another description from Paul. At Jesus' return, believers who were "asleep" in death will "rise," resurrected from their graves. Then, together with those believers who were still alive, they would rise to "meet the Lord in the air":

> **But I would not have you to be ignorant, brethren, concerning them which are asleep, that ye sorrow not, even as others which have no hope.**

For if we believe that Jesus died and rose again, even so them also which sleep in Jesus will God bring with him.

For this we say unto you by the word of the Lord, that we which are alive and remain unto the coming of the Lord shall not prevent them which are asleep.

For the Lord himself shall descend from heaven with a shout, with the voice of the archangel, and with the trump of God: and the dead in Christ shall rise first:

Then we which are alive and remain shall be caught up together with them in the clouds, to meet the Lord in the air: and so shall we ever be with the Lord (1 Thessalonians 4:13-17)

Did you notice that nothing at all was said about going to heaven, or being in heaven? There is something much more useful and meaningful in store for those who receive eternal life at Jesus' return. I'll explain this shortly.

Works

We've explored "saved" in the context of Ephesians 2:8-10. Now the part about "works" in that passage:

Again, here are all three verses:

8. For by grace are ye saved through faith; and that not of yourselves: it is the gift of God:

9. Not of works, lest any man should boast.

10. For we are his workmanship, created in

Christ Jesus unto good works, which God hath before ordained that we should walk in them (Ephesians 2:8-10)

The "works" in verse 9 refers to the good deeds or "good works" in verse 10. That's the context. Those "good works" are done by love, as a result of our becoming "his workmanship." The "new man" does good works because it is becoming his nature to do so. Those good works do not, and can not, *earn* saving grace. If they could *earn* saving grace then there would have been no need for Jesus, no need for Jesus to die for us. It is only through Jesus' death that redemption is now available for us. There is no substitute for the ransom payment Jesus made available when He died. Without His death we would all be hopelessly doomed to perish as the "wages" of our own sin. We are all sinners in need of redemption.

Speaking of "works" this would be a good place to mention that doing "the works of the law," likewise, cannot earn saving grace. The reason is the same: we are sinners in need of redemption. Redemption is only available via the ransom Jesus made available—available to cover our death penalty—when He died for us. Paul wrote that if he were to preach that saving grace came by doing the works of the law, he would "frustrate": nullify, diminish, or circumvent what Christ made available by His death:

I do not frustrate the grace of God: for if righteousness come by the law, then Christ is dead in vain (Galatians 2:21)

There is nothing we can do to *earn* saving grace. Grace is **promised** to us if we—through faith—will obey and "come to God" (Hebrews 11:6) on His terms: in repentance. Jesus is

> **. . . the author of eternal salvation unto all them that obey him (Hebrews 5:9)**

"Works" refers to different things in different contexts. We have seen "good works" and the "works" or "deeds of the law." The apostle James used Abraham's example to illustrate another kind of works: obedience to God through faith. By or through faith, Abraham chose to obey God and left for the promised land:

> **By faith Abraham, when he was called to go out into a place which he should after receive for an inheritance, obeyed; and he went out, not knowing whither he went (Hebrews 11:8)**

Can you imagine doing that? Abraham packed and left. He walked out of the gates of Ur, his city, without even knowing what direction to turn. There's an example for us today: God will show us the way to the promised land . . . IF we, through faith, will obey and step out of our "city."

Later, Abraham obeyed again when instructed to offer his son Isaac. In both cases Abraham chose to leave his comfort zone—"step off his boat"—and obey. For his "works," his obedience through faith, he was deemed to be a believer and was justified to God . . . "and not by faith only"! James wrote:

> **But wilt thou know, O vain man, that faith without works is dead?**
>
> **Was not Abraham our father justified by works, when he had offered Isaac his son upon the altar?**
>
> **Seest thou how faith wrought with his works, and by works was faith made perfect?**

And the scripture was fulfilled which saith, Abraham believed God, and it was imputed unto him for righteousness: and he was called the Friend of God.

Ye see then how that by works a man is justified, and not by faith only (James 2:20-24)

All four instances of "faith" in that passage are from the Greek word πίστις (pistis), a noun. Faith is something you have: confidence, or trust. "Believed" in that passage is from a different (albeit related) Greek word, πιστεύο (pisteuō), which is a verb. Abraham was called a believer because he took action on his faith; his faith was not dead. He obeyed. He was not justified to God "by faith only."

True believing goes beyond "faith only." Abraham acted on his faith and obeyed. For *that* he was deemed to be a believer and was justified to God.

Abraham was justified to God, but not redeemed: redemption was not possible or available until Jesus died, over a thousand years later, making His death available to cover our death penalty. When Abraham is resurrected, he will find that his redemption has been provided for. And he will find his Redeemer waiting for him.

Even with faith, Abraham could have just chosen to remain in his comfort zones. He could have chosen to remain at home, rather than leave for the promised land. That would have been death faith: faith without action, without obedience. He would never have received the promises.

James added:

For as the body without the spirit is dead, so faith without works is dead also (James 2:26)

James used Abraham's example to show that through or by faith we must choose to obey God. Abraham was justified to God by his "works," his obedience through faith. For his obedience through faith—because he acted on his faith and obeyed—he was deemed to be a believer, "and not by faith only" (James 2:24).

The same holds true today: *through* faith we *could* choose to come to God. That does not mean we *would* choose to come to God. Many choose to remain in their comfort zones, preferring the approval and the attractions of the world instead. Their faith is dead. Bottom line: they are not believers. "Faith alone" is dead.

Notice how Peter distinguished those who believe from the rest: he calls the rest—those who do not believe—the "disobedient":

Unto you therefore which believe he is precious: but unto them which be disobedient, the stone which the builders disallowed, the same is made the head of the corner,

And a stone of stumbling, and a rock of offence, even to them which stumble at the word, being disobedient: whereunto also they were appointed (1 Peter 2:7,8)

Proponents of "faith alone" are often quick to accuse those who do not subscribe to "faith alone" of being "works salvationists." "Faith alone" says, and means, "faith alone" is sufficient for the receipt of saving grace; "works" of *any* sort are unnecessary for salvation. That is error; outside of repentance—confessing and forsaking sin—our sins remain and we do not receive His promised mercy and grace. As we've seen, it is *through* faith that we might choose to come to repentance. And then, for that obedience—that repentance—we enter His promised mercy and grace. Then, through His grace, we can receive redemption, the holy spirit and finally salvation: the gift of eternal life.

"Works" refers to different things in different contexts. It is most certainly true that we can not *earn* redemption by doing "good works"; redemption is possible only by grace, through Jesus. Same holds true for the "works of the law." But to jump to the conclusion that no "works" are needed—of *any* kind—is error and leads to the errant, do-nothing theology: "faith + nothing = salvation."

Is it reasonable to think that we'd be justified to God, and then given eternal life, while remaining in un-repentance and disobedience to God? No. Of course not. It defies common sense. Yet that is the underhanded message of "faith alone." "Faith alone" means nothing other than faith is required. It's a sly, underhanded way of saying that neither repentance nor obedience are necessary!

Here's an example, recently written by a "faith alone" preacher:

> *Do you believe your a sinner, once separated from God but now forgiven by believing that Christ willingly died on the cross to remove your sins, was buried in a tomb & risen on the 3rd day?*

My comment: oops: fundamental error right there there in the first sentence. Our sins were not "removed" when Jesus died on the cross. Our sins remain—not blotted out—until and unless we come to repentance! Acts 3:19:

Repent therefore and be converted, that your sins

may be blotted out, so that times of refreshing may come from the presence of the Lord (Acts 3:19, NKJV)

Our sins were not forgiven the moment Jesus died on the cross. Our sins remain, un-forgiven. But

If we confess our sins, he is faithful and just to forgive us our sins, and to cleanse us from all unrighteousness (1 John 1:9)

"If" . . . such a small word, yet so much depends on it!

Given Jesus' warning "except ye repent, ye shall all likewise perish" (Luke 13:5) it is obvious that more is required than just trusting or "faith alone"!

The "faith alone" preacher continues:

Well... I've got some great (Biblical) news!

You are justified in the eyes of God - baptized into the Body of Christ and NOTHING can ever change that. You can't sin your way out of it, you can't not believe to the point you lose it, you nor anyone on this earth can do anything to undo what God has done the moment you have heard and believed the gospel today in this dispensation of grace we are all living in.

My comments: Wow. Just "trust"—"faith alone"—that Jesus has already removed your sins and you're instantly justified to God. No obedience necessary. No repentance necessary. In fact, he dares to say "and NOTHING can ever change that . . . You can't sin your way out of" justification. He's flat-out ignoring scripture:

Follow peace with all men, and holiness, without which no man shall see the Lord (Hebrews 12:14)

Know ye not that the unrighteous shall not inherit the kingdom of God? Be not deceived: neither fornicators, nor idolaters, nor adulterers, nor effeminate, nor abusers of themselves with mankind,

Nor thieves, nor covetous, nor drunkards, nor revilers, nor extortioners, shall inherit the kingdom of God (1 Corinthians 6:9,10; also Ephesians 5:5,6 and Galatians 5:19-21)

Why would this "faith alone" preacher say such a thing? Why would he say sin is no longer a salvation issue? Very simple: he assumes that all sins—past, present and future—were "paid for" the moment Jesus died on the cross. Therefore, he concludes, sin can no longer be a salvation issue! He concludes that repentance—turning from sin—is no longer necessary because, after all, all our sins have been "paid for"! By "faith alone" we'll even have "eternal security." Why? Because it's impossible for us to undo what has already been done for us on the cross: our sins have already been "paid in full."

That sort of reasoning is common among the easy-grace, "faith alone, instantly saved with eternal security" crowd. "Faith alone" is rooted in a gross misunderstanding of what Jesus finished on the cross. Jesus did not pay for our sins when He died on the cross: He made a payment, His blood, *available* when He died on the cross. He made His death available to cover our death penalty. We can have that coverage, that mercy, that redemption—as promised—IF we'll obey and come to repentance.

"Faith alone" preachers often try to prove "repent" has nothing to do with turning from sin. They cite the fact that God—who is not a sinner—"repented": He changed His mind about punishing Nineveh. This is often presented as evidence/proof that "repent" has nothing to do with turning from sin. Yet in most scriptural contexts "repent" is in the context of turning from sin. The very same verse they reference shows that God repented—changed His mind and had mercy—because Nineveh repented: they changed their minds about continuing in sin:

> **And God saw their works, that they turned from their evil way; and God repented of the evil, that he had said that he would do unto them; and he did it not (Jonah 3:10)**

"Faith alone" takes "repent" and redefines it according to their theology. "Faith alone" says repent means change your mind and just trust Jesus has already paid for all your sins. After you've been instantly "saved" by just trusting, you might turn from sin, but hey, since you're already "saved" anyway, it obviously isn't really necessary. Thus they relegate true repentance—turning from sin—to optional insignificance. Great news for itching ears!

"Faith alone" often insists repentance has nothing to do with turning from sin. Recently a "faith alone" person challenged me in writing:

> *Find me a verse about repentance the way you understand it after Jesus was resurrected.* ☺ *please*

I replied with the following New Testament verses:

> **And lest, when I come again, my God will humble me among you, and that I shall bewail many which have sinned already, and have not repented of the uncleanness and fornication and**

lasciviousness which they have committed (the apostle Paul, 2 Corinthians 12:21)

But Peter said unto him, Thy money perish with thee, because thou hast thought that the gift of God may be purchased with money. Thou hast neither part nor lot in this matter: for thy heart is not right in the sight of God. Repent therefore of this thy wickedness, and pray God, if perhaps the thought of thine heart may be forgiven thee (Acts 8:20-22)

And the rest of the men which were not killed by these plagues yet repented not of the works of their hands, that they should not worship devils, and idols of gold, and silver, and brass, and stone, and of wood: which neither can see, nor hear, nor walk:

Neither repented they of their murders, nor of their sorceries, nor of their fornication, nor of their thefts (Revelation 9:20,21)

And the fifth angel poured out his vial upon the seat of the beast; and his kingdom was full of darkness; and they gnawed their tongues for pain,

And blasphemed the God of heaven because of their pains and their sores, and repented not of their deeds (Rev 16:10,11)

And I gave her space to repent of her fornication; and she repented not. Behold, I will cast her into a bed, and them that commit adultery with her into great tribulation, except they repent of their deeds (Revelation 2:21,22)

And here are a few more passages, spoken by Jesus *before* His resurrection:

> Take heed to yourselves: If thy brother trespass against thee, rebuke him; and if he repent, forgive him. And if he trespass against thee seven times in a day, and seven times in a day turn again to thee, saying, I repent; thou shalt forgive him (Luke 17:3,4)

> When Jesus heard it, he saith unto them, They that are whole have no need of the physician, but they that are sick: I came not to call the righteous, but sinners to repentance (Mark 2:17)

> I say unto you, that likewise joy shall be in heaven over one sinner that repenteth, more than over ninety and nine just persons, which need no repentance (Luke 15:7)

Before we return to the "faith alone" preacher there is one more point to make about Jonah 3:10:

> And God saw their works, that they turned from their evil way; and God repented of the evil, that he had said that he would do unto them; and he did it not (Jonah 3:10)

"Faith alone" has a knee-jerk reaction to the word "works" in that verse: "Oh, see? Turning from sin is 'works,' and no one is saved by works, so no one has to turn from sin."

My response to that is simple: salvation is by God's mercy and grace. And who receives the mercy and grace? It's those who come to God on His terms, confessing and forsaking sin. Outside of repentance, we remain outside His mercy and grace, therefore we remain outside salvation.

We *are* judged by our works:

And I saw the dead, small and great, stand before God; and the books were opened: and another book was opened, which is the book of life: and the dead were judged out of those things which were written in the books, according to their works.

And the sea gave up the dead which were in it; and death and hell delivered up the dead which were in them: and they were judged every man according to their works (Revelation 20:12,13)

No repentance? No Mercy. **Perhaps the "faith alone" crowd should think about that before they dismiss Nineveh's "works" as irrelevant!**

That reminds me: Jesus had something to say about Nineveh, judgment and condemnation:

The men of Nineveh shall rise in judgment with this generation, and shall condemn it: because they repented at the preaching of Jonas; and, behold, a greater than Jonas is here (Matthew 12:41)

Outside of repentance, we face condemnation. Therefor it should be common-sense obvious that "faith alone" or "just trust" is not enough!

Okay, back to the "faith alone" preacher's words:

So, what exactly did God do the moment you heard and believed in the gospel of what Christ did for your sins? The word of God says that you have been sealed with the

Holy Spirit of promise... until you are redeemed at the rapture of the Body of Christ. Sealed, stamped and eternally secured!

My comments: More error, because no one gets the holy spirit by just trusting. God gives His spirit "to them that obey him":

And we are his witnesses of these things; and so is also the Holy Ghost, whom God hath given to them that obey him (Acts 5:32)

Obey: come to God in repentance first. Then you will receive the gift of the holy spirit:

Then Peter said unto them, Repent, and be baptized every one of you in the name of Jesus Christ for the remission of sins, and ye shall receive the gift of the Holy Ghost (Acts 2:38)

Acts 3:19 shows we must come to repentance first, then our past sins will be blotted out. Those sins had separated us from God (Isaiah 59:1,2). Now, with those sins blotted out, we enter justification: we are in right-standing with God, no longer separated. Now we can begin a new life—"times of refreshing"—in "the presence of the Lord":

Repent therefore and be converted, that your sins may be blotted out, so that times of refreshing may come from the presence of the Lord (Acts 3:19, NKJV)

And how are we in the presence of the Lord? Through the gift of the holy spirit, given to them that obey and come to Him in repentance! Through faith we may choose to come to God in repentance; for that we are promised His mercy—and we'll receive the gift of the holy spirit. We do not receive the gift of the holy spirit just because we have faith. There is such as thing as dead faith. Faith without obedience—without coming to God on His terms—is dead faith.

The "faith alone" preacher continues:

The word of God says positionally you are now IN Christ in Heavenly places (whether you know it or not), and you have been given PEACE with God! Wow... God has nothing against you.... you have been totally forgiven and have peace with God! You have been justified and given the imputed righteousness of none other than our Lord & SAVIOR Jesus Christ - by believing in HIS faithfulness and what He accomplished on that cross.

Can I get an Amen?! It's because we simply heard and trusted in the gospel of what Christ did for us. Some say once saved - always saved.... hyper grace.... eternally secured.... I just call it simply trusting Gods word, and rightly dividing the scriptures - studying to show ourselves approved and believing His word. Eternally secured, justified, righteous, forgiven, perfected, sealed - and it's all because I trusted in what Jesus did for me!

My comments: No, it's not "all because I trusted in what Jesus did for me." We get the mercy—as promised—if we'll obey and "come to God" (Hebrews 11:6), confessing and forsaking sin (Proverbs 28:13). Then our past sins will be blotted out (Acts 3:19) and we'll receive the gift of the holy spirit (Acts 2:38). With the holy spirit we can begin a new life: the "times of refreshing" in "the presence of the Lord" mentioned in Acts 3:19. "Just trust" is just wishful thinking.

Part 1: The Basics

Creation Is Not Finished

The original creation was done through or by the "Word," who later appeared in the flesh as Jesus:

> In the beginning was the Word, and the Word was with God, and the Word was God.
>
> The same was in the beginning with God.
>
> All things were made by him; and without him was not any thing made that was made . . .
>
> And the Word was made flesh, and dwelt among us, (and we beheld his glory, the glory as of the only begotten of the Father,) full of grace and truth (John 1:1-3,14)

This is confirmed throughout the New Testament:

> And to make all men see what is the fellowship of the mystery, which from the beginning of the world hath been hid in God, who created all things by Jesus Christ (Ephesians 3:9)
>
> For by him were all things created, that are in heaven, and that are in earth, visible and invisible, whether they be thrones, or dominions, or principalities, or powers: all things were created by him, and for him:
>
> And he is before all things, and by him all things consist.
>
> And he is the head of the body, the church: who is the beginning, the firstborn from the dead; that in all things he might have the preeminence (Colossians 1:16–18)

> **God, who at sundry times and in divers manners spake in time past unto the fathers by the prophets,**
>
> **Hath in these last days spoken unto us by his Son, whom he hath appointed heir of all things, by whom also he made the worlds (Hebrews 1:1,2)**

Jesus' work is not finished: creation is not finished. Through the holy spirit Jesus guides us and helps us overcome slavery to sin. He leads us into His righteousness. This is how we are made ready to receive the gift of eternal life and to inherit the Kingdom of God. Creation is still in process: sons and daughters for the Father's eternal family are being created, right now, through Jesus. He is the potter, we are the clay. Jesus says:

> **As many as I love, I rebuke and chasten: be zealous therefore, and repent (Revelation 3:19)**

Jesus does not force us to follow His lead; we must choose to follow the lead He provides through the holy spirit. This requires our ongoing repentance, abiding in Him. Only by abiding in Him in repentance can we be become "his workmanship" (Ephesians 2:10), re-shaped like clay into the "new man" we saw back in Ephesians 4.

Here is Paul, showing we must choose to be *led* by the holy spirit; we can not do that unless we remain in repentance:

> **For if ye live after the flesh, ye shall die: but if ye through the Spirit do mortify the deeds of the body, ye shall live.**
>
> **For as many as are led by the Spirit of God, they are the sons of God (Romans 8:13,14)**

Part 1: The Basics

A relationship with Him

> . . . yieldeth the peaceable fruit of righteousness unto them which are exercised thereby (Hebrews 12:11)

Jesus says:

> He that hath an ear, let him hear what the Spirit saith unto the churches; To him that overcometh will I give to eat of the tree of life, which is in the midst of the paradise of God (Revelation 2:7)

> He that hath an ear, let him hear what the Spirit saith unto the churches; He that overcometh shall not be hurt of the second death (Revelation 2:11)

> He that overcometh, the same shall be clothed in white raiment; and I will not blot out his name out of the book of life, but I will confess his name before my Father, and before his angels (Revelation 3:5)

> He that overcometh shall inherit all things; and I will be his God, and he shall be my son (Revelation 21:7)

I hope you can appreciate the contrast between those verses and the "faith alone" narrative, which says "He that hath faith alone shall inherit all things; and I will be his God, and he shall be my son." The "faith alone, instantly saved" paradigm is a tacit denial of any need to overcome. It omits sanctification altogether because if you're instantly "saved" and have "eternal security" upon "faith alone" then by implication there no need for sanctification . . . no need to overcome. No need to do *anything*!

God's calling can be likened to a race in which everyone who finishes is a winner. Without faith, we never "see" that there *is* a race, so we can not and do not enter the race. With faith, we see there is a race we may enter. Without repentance, we can not enter or start the race. Entering the race does not mean the race is finished; we must run in order to finish. Without abiding in Him in ongoing repentance we are not running the race. We must endure or run to the end to finish the race. Then we'll win salvation, the promised gift of eternal life. We'll have victory over death.

We can not make the journey along the "narrow way" (Matthew 7:14) that leads to eternal life without His help. And that journey can neither begin nor continue without our repentance, abiding in Him. He KNOWS we need His help; He IS ready to help us. He gave His LIFE so that we—if we'll come to repentance—could be redeemed from the death penalty already earned for past sins. And as long as we remain in repentance, abiding in Him, we are walking "in the light." We'll remain in His grace and His blood will continue to cover our sins when they occur:

> **But if we walk in the light, as he is in the light, we have fellowship one with another, and the blood of Jesus Christ his Son cleanseth us from all sin (1 John 1:7)**

"Cleanseth" is active, present tense. Were all our sins, "past present and future," blotted out when Jesus died on the cross? No! Our past sins will be blotted out *if we'll come to repentance.* While we remain in repentance, new sins we might commit will also be blotted out, washed away.

Part 1: The Basics

"You're a Works Salvationist!"

Those who preach "faith alone" have invented their own false dichotomy, saying that anything other than "faith alone" must therefore be "works salvation": an attempt to *earn* salvation by works, by our own efforts. For example, by doing good works or by doing "the works of the law."

That's a lame, tired, straw man argument. First of all, neither salvation nor justification are by "faith alone." Salvation is by God's grace:

> **For by grace are ye saved through faith; and that not of yourselves: it is the gift of God (Ephesians 2:8)**

The question of the day is, *"**Who gets the mercy and grace?**"*

Mercy and grace are *promised*, not *earned*. Those who—through faith—obey and come to Him on His terms, in repentance, are promised mercy:

> **And the times of this ignorance God winked at; but now commandeth all men every where to repent (Acts 17:30)**

> **He that covereth his sins shall not prosper: but whoso confesseth and forsaketh them shall have mercy (Proverbs 28:13)**

> **Let the wicked forsake his way, and the unrighteous man his thoughts: and let him return unto the LORD, and he will have mercy upon him . . . (Isaiah 55:7)**

"Faith alone" says we receive mercy and grace by just by "trusting," by "faith alone." That's gross error, a mischievous lie promoted by 16th century theologians. "Faith alone" is a sneaky, underhanded way of saying that neither repentance nor obedience are required!

Jesus told His disciples to preach "repentance and remission of sins." Not "faith alone." Not "faith + nothing = salvation":

> **Then opened he their understanding, that they might understand the scriptures,**
>
> **And said unto them, Thus it is written, and thus it behoved Christ to suffer, and to rise from the dead the third day:**
>
> **And that repentance and remission of sins should be preached in his name among all nations, beginning at Jerusalem (Luke 24:45-47)**

Those who preach "faith alone" are preaching a false gospel. Jesus is "the author of eternal salvation unto all them that obey him" (Hebrews 5:9). Nothing there about "faith alone."

Outside of repentance we will perish:

> **The Lord is not slack concerning his promise, as some men count slackness; but is longsuffering to us-ward, not willing that any should perish, but that all should come to repentance (2 Peter 3:9)**

Nothing there about "faith alone," either. "Faith alone" is a seductive and dangerous perversion of the gospel.

Part Two: Eternal Security

"Once Saved, Always Saved"

Let's go back to the "faith alone" preacher's closing words:

Can I get an Amen?! It's because we simply heard and trusted in the gospel of what Christ did for us. Some say once saved - always saved.... hyper grace.... eternally secured.... I just call it simply trusting Gods word, and rightly dividing the scriptures - studying to show ourselves approved and believing His word. Eternally secured, justified, righteous, forgiven, perfected, sealed - and it's all because I trusted in what Jesus did for me!

Makes me ill just reading it. The "narrow way" that few find becomes an instant arrival at the end of easy street.

We have free will. We are not forced to abide in Him, nor are we forced to continue in repentance. We must choose to be led by the holy spirit, as we saw earlier. Some theologians say the holy spirit *makes* you repent, as if it overrides your free will. Theologians call this *monergism*. Nice try: that also makes it the holy spirit's fault—God's fault—if you don't repent. Monergism is nothing more than a convenient theological way to excuse yourself from personal responsibility to come to repentance.

It *is* possible for us fail to abide in Him. We really can return to un-repentance. We have many warnings from Jesus and the apostles NOT TO LET THAT HAPPEN!

But the wolf says "No, no, no: you're saved and safe . . . there is no danger . . . no harm can come to you." Massive deception is going on. Spiritual warfare is raging and most don't realize it. Bottom line, the "faith alone, instantly saved, eternally secure" paradigm defies the many warnings provided in scripture. I'll list some of those warnings below, with comments.

Warnings

If "eternal security" or "once saved, always saved" were true, then there would have been no point in warnings like these:

If a man abide not in me, he is cast forth as a branch, and is withered; and men gather them, and cast them into the fire, and they are burned (Jesus, in John 15:6)

You can't be "cast off as a branch" without first becoming a branch. You *can* be "cast off as a branch" after becoming a branch. Jesus did not say "once a branch, always a branch." It's amazing to me that anyone could conclude you're still "saved" after being "cast off as a branch" and "withered" and "cast into the fire" and "burned." Simply amazing. Even so, many insist they would be "saved," anyway.

The apostle Paul warned that believers, even after being "graffed" into the "vine," could be "cut off" the vine, just as the "natural branches" (the Israelites) had been broken off:

Thou wilt say then, The branches were broken

> off, that I might be graffed in.
>
> Well; because of unbelief they were broken off, and thou standest by faith. Be not highminded, but fear:
>
> For if God spared not the natural branches, take heed lest he also spare not thee.
>
> Behold therefore the goodness and severity of God: on them which fell, severity; but toward thee, goodness, if thou continue in his goodness: otherwise thou also shalt be cut off (Romans 11:19-22)

"If thou continue in his goodness: otherwise thou also shalt be cut off" . . . compare that to the "faith alone" preacher's "You are justified in the eyes of God - baptized into the Body of Christ and NOTHING can ever change that. You can't sin your way out of it, you can't not believe to the point you lose it . . ."

And there's that "if" again . . . "if thou continue in His goodness," His grace. It is painfully obvious that we can fail to "continue in his goodness." We should "fear" and "take heed" not to let that happen. And if we allow that to happen, we'll be "cut off." That does not mean "saved, anyway." Amazingly, though, you'll find folks that say you're "saved anyway," no matter what. The word *delusional* comes to mind.

> Let us therefore fear, lest, a promise being left us of entering into his rest, any of you should seem to come short of it (Hebrews 4:1)

Obviously we really CAN come short of entering into his rest. And that is something to be feared.

The apostle Paul clearly refuted "once saved, always saved": he stated he could become a "castaway":

> **But I keep under my body, and bring it into subjection: lest that by any means, when I have preached to others, I myself should be a castaway (1 Corinthians 9:27)**

Yes, Paul understood that even after preaching to others it was still possible for him to be a "castaway" . . . rejected and disposed of.

Even after overcoming slavery to sin through knowing Jesus, it is still possible to return to a life of sin. In that case "the latter end is worse with them than the beginning":

> **For if after they have escaped the pollutions of the world through the knowledge of the Lord and Saviour Jesus Christ, they are again entangled therein, and overcome, the latter end is worse with them than the beginning.**
>
> **For it had been better for them not to have known the way of righteousness, than, after they have known it, to turn from the holy commandment delivered unto them.**
>
> **But it is happened unto them according to the true proverb, The dog is turned to his own vomit again; and the sow that was washed to her wallowing in the mire (2 Peter 2:20-22)**

Here is a similar warning about willfully returning to a life if sin:

> **For if we sin wilfully after that we have received the knowledge of the truth, there remaineth no**

more sacrifice for sins,

But a certain fearful looking for of judgment and fiery indignation, which shall devour the adversaries (Hebrews 10:26,27)

It *is* possible to "fall away" from justification, even after receiving—being made a "partaker"—of the holy spirit! There would have been no point in writing the next passage if it were impossible to fall away:

For it is impossible for those who were once enlightened, and have tasted of the heavenly gift, and were made partakers of the Holy Ghost,

And have tasted the good word of God, and the powers of the world to come,

If they shall fall away, to renew them again unto repentance; seeing they crucify to themselves the Son of God afresh, and put him to an open shame (Hebrews 6:4-6)

We can "fail of the grace of God":

Follow peace with all men, and holiness, without which no man shall see the Lord:

Looking diligently lest any man fail of the grace of God; lest any root of bitterness springing up trouble you, and thereby many be defiled (Hebrews 12:14,15)

Our names CAN be blotted out of the book of life:

He that overcometh, the same shall be clothed in white raiment; and I will not blot out his name out of the book of life, but I will confess his name before my Father, and before his an-

gels (Revelation 3:5)

Here's another example of "if" with conditions:

Wherefore the rather, brethren, give diligence to make your calling and election sure: for if ye do these things, ye shall never fall:

For so an entrance shall be ministered unto you abundantly into the everlasting kingdom of our Lord and Saviour Jesus Christ (2 Peter 1:10,11)

We are urged to "give diligence to make our calling and election sure"—not to coast along presuming we're already "saved"!

Another "if" with conditions:

Take heed, brethren, lest there be in any of you an evil heart of unbelief, in departing from the living God.

But exhort one another daily, while it is called To day; lest any of you be hardened through the deceitfulness of sin.

For we are made partakers of Christ, if we hold the beginning of our confidence stedfast unto the end (Hebrews 3:12-14)

Another "if" with conditions:

And you, that were sometime alienated and enemies in your mind by wicked works, yet now hath he reconciled

In the body of his flesh through death, to present you holy and unblameable and unreproveable in his sight:

> If ye continue in the faith grounded and settled, and be not moved away from the hope of the gospel, which ye have heard, and which was preached to every creature which is under heaven; whereof I Paul am made a minister (Colossians 1:21-23)

More "ifs":

> For if ye live after the flesh, ye shall die: but if ye through the Spirit do mortify the deeds of the body, ye shall live.
>
> For as many as are led by the Spirit of God, they are the sons of God (Romans 8:13,14)

Jesus clearly warned what would happen to servants who returned to sin:

> But and if that servant say in his heart, My lord delayeth his coming; and shall begin to beat the menservants and maidens, and to eat and drink, and to be drunken;
>
> The lord of that servant will come in a day when he looketh not for him, and at an hour when he is not aware, and will cut him in sunder, and will appoint him his portion with the unbelievers (Luke 12:45,46)

That servant was going to pay for his sins himself! "Once saved, always saved," with "eternal security"? Apparently not. Sins "all paid for, past, present and future"? Apparently not.

If that "faith alone" preacher were "simply trusting Gods word" as he claims, he'd take these warnings seriously. It is entirely possible for us to reject the lead provided by the holy spirit, no longer abiding in Jesus. Even after receiving the holy spirit and knowing Jesus, we can fall away, returning to a life of un-repentance and sin. Then we'll be outside His mercy, just as we were before coming to Him. We will have fallen away from justification and returned to condemnation. We will have "failed of the grace of God." We are urged to "give diligence" not to let that happen. If we let it happen, then we'll no longer be "in his goodness," His grace. Outside His grace, our "hope of salvation" is gone, forfeited. Ultimately we'll be "cut off"; "cast . . . into the fire, and . . . burned" . . . a "castaway."

In spite of all these warnings, many still insist that they have been "saved" and that they have "eternal security": "once saved, always saved." Trouble is, they are not saved: unless they receive the gift of eternal life, at Jesus' return, they will perish, losing everything, very much unsaved. Only upon the receipt of eternal life will anyone have eternal security.

In this mortal life we may enter justification:

There is therefore now no condemnation to them which are in Christ Jesus, who walk not after the flesh, but after the Spirit (Romans 8:1)

And while we remain in justification we remain "in his goodness"—in His grace—and we have "the hope of salvation." So, what happens if we no longer abide in Him in repentance, no longer walking "after the spirit"? We return to condemnation, no longer in justification. No longer in His "goodness" or grace, we will be "cut off." We will have forfeited our "hope of salvation." We will no longer be "appointed . . . to obtain salvation" (1 Thessalonians 5:8,9).

Part 2: Eternal Security

Twisted Verses

Those who insist they have eternal security are denying that it is possible to fall away from justification, despite all the scriptures that indicate otherwise. They will quote scripture in an attempt to prove their point, but their alleged "proofs" are empty. For example, "sealed" in Ephesians 1:13,14 is often cited as proof of eternal security:

> **In whom ye also trusted, after that ye heard the word of truth, the gospel of your salvation: in whom also after that ye believed, ye were sealed with that holy Spirit of promise,**
>
> **Which is the earnest of our inheritance until the redemption of the purchased possession, unto the praise of his glory (Ephesians 1:13,14)**

The sequence of events is the same as we've seen. After hearing "the word of truth, the gospel" they "trusted": they had faith. They chose to act on their faith: they "believed"—they obeyed and came to God on His terms, in repentance. Then they received the holy spirit. The fact that they had received the holy spirit was a sign, an "earnest," to each of them personally. Receipt of the holy spirit assured them that they were marked or designated to receive an inheritance: the Kingdom of God. They were to receive that inheritance upon "the redemption of the purchased possession," referring to their resurrection with a new and immortal spiritual body in place of their mortal, physical body.

Incidentally, this handshakes with Paul's statement that as flesh and blood mortals can not inherit the kingdom; we must first receive an immortal, spirit body:

> Now this I say, brethren, that flesh and blood cannot inherit the kingdom of God; neither doth corruption inherit incorruption.
>
> Behold, I shew you a mystery; We shall not all sleep, but we shall all be changed,
>
> In a moment, in the twinkling of an eye, at the last trump: for the trumpet shall sound, and the dead shall be raised incorruptible, and we shall be changed.
>
> For this corruptible must put on incorruption, and this mortal must put on immortality (1 Corinthians 15:50-53)

As we saw earlier, we must choose to be led by the holy spirit:

> For if ye live after the flesh, ye shall die: but if ye through the Spirit do mortify the deeds of the body, ye shall live.
>
> For as many as are led by the Spirit of God, they are the sons of God (Romans 8:13,14)

This requires our ongoing repentance. The holy spirit does not and can not force us to follow. Even after knowing Jesus we can choose to revert back to a life of sin, no longer in repentance, no longer abiding in Him. Then, as Peter warned, "the latter end of them is worse than the beginning":

> For if after they have escaped the pollutions of the world through the knowledge of the Lord and Saviour Jesus Christ, they are again entangled therein, and overcome, the latter end is worse

with them than the beginning.

For it had been better for them not to have known the way of righteousness, than, after they have known it, to turn from the holy commandment delivered unto them.

But it is happened unto them according to the true proverb, The dog is turned to his own vomit again; and the sow that was washed to her wallowing in the mire. (2 Peter 2:20-22)

Ephesians 4:30 also mentions being sealed:

And grieve not the holy Spirit of God, whereby ye are sealed unto the day of redemption (Ephesians 4:30. 2 Corinthians 1:22 and 5:5 are similar)

No one should assume that *having* holy spirit is proof that you *have been* "saved," done deal. Nor should anyone assume that having the holy spirit is a guarantee that you *will be* saved. Such assumptions blatantly deny all the warnings to abide in Him and remain in His "goodness," or else be "cut off" and "burned." Such assumptions deny that any of those "ifs" quoted earlier even exist. But they do exist: they're written in black and white to warn us.

Did the apostle Paul have the holy spirit? Yes. Did he preach that he was sealed or guaranteed to have salvation? No. He knew it was possible to revert to a life of sin and therefore be rejected . . . a "castaway":

But I keep under my body, and bring it into subjection: lest that by any means, when I have preached to others, I myself should be a castaway (1 Corinthians 9:27)

John 6:37 is another verse often cited as proof of eternal security:

All that the Father giveth me shall come to me; and him that cometh to me I will in no wise cast out.

Unfortunately many see the words "I will in no wise cast out" and jump to the conclusion no one will be "cast out," therefore—voilà—they have eternal security.

Not so fast. The verse says all *who come to Him* He will not cast out. What happens if we choose to no longer come to Him? If we deny Him, and choose to no longer abide in Him? Here's the answer:

If we suffer, we shall also reign with him: if we deny him, he also will deny us (2 Timothy 2:12)

If a man abide not in me, he is cast forth as a branch, and is withered; and men gather them, and cast them into the fire, and they are burned (Jesus, in John 15:6)

That does not mean "saved, anyway." Continuing in John chapter 6:

For I came down from heaven, not to do mine own will, but the will of him that sent me.

And this is the Father's will which hath sent me, that of all which he hath given me I should lose nothing, but should raise it up again at the last day (John 6:38,39)

"Eternal security" puts a spin on the passage, saying it means none will be lost. No: the passage says it's the Father's will—His desire and intention—that no one be lost.

Part 2: Eternal Security

Men have been defying God's will since the beginning, and will continue to do so until the end. It's the Father's *will* that no one should perish, but the will of many is to travel the wide, easy road that leads to destruction rather than the narrow way that leads to life. Even after believing—taking the "narrow way"—we can depart from it, and we are warned not to let that happen.

The Lord's will—His desire or intention—is that all men come to repentance rather than perish:

The Lord is not slack concerning his promise, as some men count slackness; but is longsuffering to us-ward, not willing that any should perish, but that all should come to repentance (2 Peter 3:9)

The Lord's will—His desire or intention—is that all should be saved and come to the knowledge of the truth:

Who will have all men to be saved, and to come unto the knowledge of the truth (1 Timothy 2:4)

Unfortunately most will not be saved. Instead, they will choose the wide, easy way that leads to destruction:

Enter ye in at the strait gate: for wide is the gate, and broad is the way, that leadeth to destruction, and many there be which go in thereat

Because strait is the gate, and narrow is the way, which leadeth unto life, and few there be that find it (Matthew 7:13,14)

Continuing in John chapter 6:

And this is the will of him that sent me, that every one which seeth the Son, and believeth on him, may have everlasting life: and I will raise

him up at the last day (John 6:40)

It's the Father's will—His desire or intention—that those who believe on Jesus would be saved. As we've seen, true believers—like Abraham—are those who act on their faith and obey God (Hebrews 11:8; James 2:20-24). Through faith they choose to come to God (Hebrews 11:6), confessing and forsaking sin. For that they receive His promised mercy and enter into His grace. If they "continue in his goodness"—His grace, (Romans 11:22), they shall be saved, in the future.

Here's Peter speaking to apostles and elders about future salvation for both themselves and Gentiles:

But we believe that through the grace of the Lord Jesus Christ we shall be saved, even as they (Acts 15:11)

Peter did not tell them they *had been* saved.

Here are another two verses often quoted as proof of "eternal security":

Now unto him that is able to keep you from falling, and to present you faultless before the presence of his glory with exceeding joy (Jude 1:24)

Philippians 1:6 is similar:

Being confident of this very thing, that he which hath begun a good work in you will perform it until the day of Jesus Christ (Philippians 1:6)

We are not kept on leashes. Jesus will keep us only if we are coming to Him, willing to be kept! If we choose to walk away, no longer abiding in Him, no longer in repentance, then He cannot work with us. Ultimately we'll be "cast off" as branches, and "cast . . . into the fire, and . . . burned." "If we deny Him, He also will deny us" (2 Timothy 2:12)

In spite of those warnings, Romans 8 verses 38 and 39 are often cited as proof that we can't possibly be separated from God:

> **For I am persuaded, that neither death, nor life, nor angels, nor principalities, nor powers, nor things present, nor things to come,**
>
> **Nor height, nor depth, nor any other creature, shall be able to separate us from the love of God, which is in Christ Jesus our Lord (Romans 8:38,39)**

Nothing *else* can separate us from God, but we ourselves can choose to separate, to no longer abide in Him. "If we deny him, he also will deny us" (2 Timothy 2:12)

We do have free will. We must choose to follow the lead He provides through the holy spirit. He does not and will not *make* you follow the holy spirit: we must choose to follow. Outside of repentance, we're not open to being led. Jesus urges us to repent and to follow His lead. We have a responsibility to follow. Jesus says:

> **As many as I love, I rebuke and chasten: be zealous therefore, and repent (Jesus, in Revelation 3:19)**

IF we'll come to Him in repentance, we'll *enter* His grace. As we remain in repentance, abiding in Him, we *remain* in His grace. Jesus will continue to be our advocate at the Father's throne:

> **My little children, these things write I unto you,**

> that ye sin not. And if any man sin, we have an advocate with the Father, Jesus Christ the righteous:
>
> And he is the propitiation for our sins: and not for ours only, but also for the sins of the whole world (1 John 2:1,2)

Jesus is the propitiation for our sins: He is the means by which the penalty for our sins can be covered. That coverage, that mercy, is promised to all who come to Him in repentance. Note that the verse does not say Jesus was—past tense—the propitiation for our sins. Our sins were neither blotted out nor paid for when He died on the cross. He made coverage—propitiation—available when He died on the cross. That coverage is available when we come to repentance . . . and as we continue—present tense—in repentance.

Galatians 3:6 is often quoted as proof that "works"—of any sort, including obedience and repentance—do not matter . . . all you have to do, they say, is "believe" as in "just trust" or "have faith alone."

> Even as Abraham believed God, and it was accounted to him for righteousness (Galatians 3:6)

The apostle James makes it clear: Abraham was deemed a believer "not by faith only": Abraham chose to obey God, through faith. That obedience was his "works": he acted on his faith. For *that* he was deemed to be a believer and was justified to God:

> But wilt thou know, O vain man, that faith without works is dead?
>
> Was not Abraham our father justified by works,

> when he had offered Isaac his son upon the altar?
>
> Seest thou how faith wrought with his works, and by works was faith made perfect?
>
> And the scripture was fulfilled which saith, Abraham believed God, and it was imputed unto him for righteousness: and he was called the Friend of God.
>
> Ye see then how that by works a man is justified, and not by faith only (James 2:20-24)

Writing to the believers in Rome, Paul makes some statements that seem to directly contradict James:

> For if Abraham were justified by works, he hath whereof to glory; but not before God.
>
> For what saith the scripture? Abraham believed God, and it was counted unto him for righteousness.
>
> Now to him that worketh is the reward not reckoned of grace, but of debt.
>
> But to him that worketh not, but believeth on him that justifieth the ungodly, his faith is counted for righteousness.
>
> Even as David also describeth the blessedness of the man, unto whom God imputeth righteousness without works,
>
> Saying, Blessed are they whose iniquities are forgiven, and whose sins are covered. (Romans 4:2-7)

James says we're justified by works ... Paul says we're not justified by works. So, how do we resolve what seems to be a contradiction between Paul and James? Context! James and Paul are referring to different "works"! The "works" Paul referred to was "the deeds of the law." That context was established twice a few verses earlier:

> **Therefore by the deeds of the law there shall no flesh be justified in his sight: for by the law is the knowledge of sin. (Romans 3:20)**

> **Therefore we conclude that a man is justified by faith without the deeds of the law. (Romans 3:28)**

"Works" refers to different things in different contexts. In James, "works" was Abraham's obedience by or through faith ... nothing to do with the works or "deeds of the law" and nothing to do with "good works" as mentioned in Ephesians 2:10.

Paul is in agreement with James. James wrote that righteousness was imputed to Abraham because—by or through faith—he believed: he acted on his faith and obeyed. Paul says the same: righteousness is "upon all them that believe," by or through faith:

> **But now the righteousness of God without the law is manifested, being witnessed by the law and the prophets;**

> **Even the righteousness of God which is by faith of Jesus Christ unto all and upon all them that believe: for there is no difference (Romans 3:21,22)**

Part Three: Other Doctrines

After Death, What Happens?

Perhaps you're wondering about those who have presumably gone to heaven. If the "dead in Christ" are waiting for their resurrection from the grave at Jesus' return, are they somehow in heaven until then? And if they've gone to heaven, what would they need a resurrection for?

Have you have been taught that people like Abraham, David and Moses have gone to heaven? It's not true. Not one of them has gone to heaven. They are all still dead, in their graves. They have not gone to heaven. Take Jesus' word for it: no one, other than Jesus, has gone to heaven:

> **And no man hath ascended up to heaven, but he that came down from heaven, even the Son of man which is in heaven (Jesus, in John 3:13)**

Abraham, David and the others are still in the grave. The apostle Peter confirmed this when he spoke about David:

> **Men and brethren, let me freely speak unto you of the patriarch David, that he is both dead and buried, and his sepulchre is with us unto this day (Acts 2:29)**

> **For David is not ascended into the heavens: but he saith himself, The LORD said unto my Lord, Sit thou on my right hand,**

> **Until I make thy foes thy footstool (Acts 2:34,35)**

Abraham, David, Moses and the others are still in the grave, waiting for the promised resurrection. Only Jesus has gone to heaven.

When You Die

So, what happens when you give up your last breath and die? You go to the grave. There you stay until you are resurrected:

> **His breath goeth forth, he returneth to his earth; in that very day his thoughts perish (Psalm 146:4)**

While you remain in the grave, you know nothing and are unaware of the passage of time:

> **For the living know that they shall die: but the dead know not any thing, neither have they any more a reward; for the memory of them is forgotten (Ecclesiastes 9:5)**

Many times the Bible refers to death as a figurative "sleep." The dead are "asleep" in death, unaware of what is going on. Jesus referred to Lazarus as being asleep, dead, before He resurrected him:

> **These things said he: and after that he saith unto them, Our friend Lazarus sleepeth; but I go, that I may awake him out of sleep.**

> **Then said his disciples, Lord, if he sleep, he shall do well.**

> **Howbeit Jesus spake of his death: but they thought that he had spoken of taking of rest in sleep.**

> **Then said Jesus unto them plainly, Lazarus is dead (John 11:11-14)**

In Daniel 12:2 we have this reference to the dead and their resurrection:

> **And many of them that sleep in the dust of the earth shall awake, some to everlasting life, and some to shame and everlasting contempt.**

"Absent From the Body..."

On the surface, Paul's statements about preferring "to be absent from the body, and to be present with the Lord" and "to depart, and to be with Christ" seem to contradict waiting in the grave for your resurrection. Here are those two passages from Paul:

> **We are confident, I say, and willing rather to be absent from the body, and to be present with the Lord (2 Corinthians 5:8)**

> **For I am in a strait betwixt two, having a desire to depart, and to be with Christ; which is far better (Philippians 1:23)**

Paul understood that upon death a man's "thoughts perish"—his consciousness stops:

> **His breath goeth forth, he returneth to his earth; in that very day his thoughts perish (Psalm 146:4)**

When the elect who "sleep in Jesus" are resurrected at Jesus' return their consciousness returns. Then—along with the elect "which are alive and remain unto the coming of the Lord"—they rise to meet Christ "in the air." Nowhere does the Bible say they meet Christ before then.

To those resurrected, it will seem like no time had passed since their last conscious moment at death. Paul understood that after his death, the very next thing he would know would be that he had been resurrected and was meeting Christ. That seemingly immediate meeting with Christ was what Paul was referring to when he wrote:

> **For I am in a strait betwixt two, having a desire to depart, and to be with Christ; which is far better (Philippians 1:23)**

Paul was confident and willing to die, knowing that as soon as he died the next thing he would know would be that he was rising to meet Christ:

> **We are confident, I say, and willing rather to be absent from the body, and to be present with the Lord (2 Corinthians 5:8)**

Paul was not a hypocrite, believing he would go to meet Jesus at the moment of his death, but telling the Thessalonians that they would have to wait for their resurrection at Jesus' return before they could meet Jesus. No; Paul wrote that he hoped to attain the very same resurrection he told the Thessalonians about:

> **That I may know him, and the power of his resurrection, and the fellowship of his sufferings, being made conformable unto his death;**
>
> **If by any means I might attain unto the resurrection of the dead (Philippians 3:10,11)**

Part 3: Other Doctrines

Resurrections

In both the Old and the New Testaments we have examples of people being raised from death back to mortal life. For example, Elijah raised the widow's son (1 Kings 17:17-24) and Jesus raised Lazarus (John 11:1-44). Those resurrections were not for the purpose of eternal reward or judgment.

There are two occasions when many will be resurrected for reward or judgment. The first occasion is only for those "in Christ" and takes place when Jesus returns. We have read Paul's descriptions of that resurrection in 1 Corinthians 15:50-54 and 1 Thessalonians 4:13-17. They are raised immortal. Revelation 20:6 describes those in this "first resurrection":

> **Blessed and holy is he that hath part in the first resurrection: on such the second death hath no power, but they shall be priests of God and of Christ, and shall reign with him a thousand years (Revelation 20:6)**

The "thousand years" refers to Jesus' rule in the Kingdom of God right here on earth, beginning at His return.

The apostle Paul described Jesus as the "firstfruits": the first to be raised immortal after death. He was "the firstborn from the dead":

> **And he is the head of the body, the church: who is the beginning, the firstborn from the dead; that in all things he might have the preeminence (Colossians 1:18)**

Those "in Christ" will follow: at Jesus' return they too will receive the gift of immortality:

But every man in his own order: Christ the firstfruits; afterward they that are Christ's at his coming (1 Corinthians 15:23)

So, what happens to the rest of the dead?

There will be another resurrection, of everyone else left in the grave, many years later:

But the rest of the dead lived not again until the thousand years were finished . . . (Revelation 20:5)

Jesus described this final resurrection:

Marvel not at this: for the hour is coming, in the which all that are in the graves shall hear his voice,

And shall come forth; they that have done good, unto the resurrection of life; and they that have done evil, unto the resurrection of damnation (Jesus, in John 5:28,29; also see Daniel 12:2).

Just to clarify, a person can be resurrected either to mortal life, or, to immortal life. Jesus resurrected Lazarus (John 11:1-44) to mortal life. Later on, Lazarus died and he is still dead, in the grave, waiting for his resurrection for reward or judgment. Martha, Lazarus' sister, understood that Lazarus would be raised again, "at the last day":

Then said Martha unto Jesus, Lord, if thou hadst been here, my brother had not died.

But I know, that even now, whatsoever thou wilt

ask of God, God will give it thee.

Jesus saith unto her, Thy brother shall rise again.

Martha saith unto him, I know that he shall rise again in the resurrection at the last day (John 11:21-24)

Martha trusted that her brother could be raised back to mortal life—immediately—if Jesus asked the Father. Jesus felt Martha and her sister Mary's sorrow over their brother's death. Jesus wept, and asked, and Lazarus rose.

Over a thousand years before Jesus, Job understood that he would wait in the grave until he was called and resurrected. Then his "change"—to immortality—would come:

O that thou wouldest hide me in the grave, that thou wouldest keep me secret, until thy wrath be past, that thou wouldest appoint me a set time, and remember me!

If a man die, shall he live again? all the days of my appointed time will I wait, till my change come.

Thou shalt call, and I will answer thee: thou wilt have a desire to the work of thine hands (Job 14:13–15)

Jesus was the first to be resurrected immortal. Those in the resurrection at Jesus' return will be resurrected immortal, like Jesus. In the last resurrection, after the 1000 years, it is evident that some are raised mortal, to "damnation" and "contempt." Others are raised to eternal life; apparently these would be people who died "in Christ" during the 1000 years.

In Paradise the Same Day?

In Luke 23:43 Jesus spoke to a thief crucified nearby. What Jesus said seems to contradict all these verses about waiting for a resurrection. It seems to suggest that instantly upon death—same day—we go to our final reward:

And Jesus said unto him, Verily I say unto thee, To day shalt thou be with me in paradise (Luke 23:43, KJV)

However Jesus was in the tomb for the next three days and three nights, as He said He would be:

For as Jonas was three days and three nights in the whale's belly; so shall the Son of man be three days and three nights in the heart of the earth (Matthew 12:40)

Even after His resurrection three days later He told Mary that He had not yet ascended to the Father:

Jesus saith unto her, Touch me not; for I am not yet ascended to my Father: but go to my brethren, and say unto them, I ascend unto my Father, and your Father; and to my God, and your God (John 20:17)

While in the tomb He was dead. He said so many years later:

I am he that liveth, and was dead; and, behold, I am alive for evermore, Amen; and have the keys of hell and of death (Revelation 1:18)

Was Jesus somehow in paradise and dead in the tomb at the same time? Of course not.

So, what's the explanation? In the original texts there were no punctuation marks, like commas, as we have today. The commas in Luke 23:43 were added by later transcribers and translators. The second comma was added in the wrong place, giving the impression Jesus and the thief would be in paradise the same day:

> **And Jesus said unto him, Verily I say unto thee, To day shalt thou be with me in paradise (Luke 23:43, KJV)**

Today some Bibles have the second comma in the correct place, immediately removing any suggestion that Jesus and the thief would be in paradise the same day. Here's some examples:

> **And Jesus said to him, "Truly, I tell you today, you shall be with Me in paradise (Faithful Version)**

> **And יהושע said to him, "Truly, I say to you today, you shall be with Me in paradise" (The Scriptures 2009)**

The following English translation of the Curetonian Syriac text even leaves out the comma in question and still delivers the correct meaning:

> **Amen, I say to thee to-day that with me thou shalt be in the Garden of Eden (F. C. Burkitt, "The Curetonian Version of the Four Gospels," Vol. I, Cambridge, 1904)**

Jesus was in the tomb three days and three nights, just as He said He would be. The thief is still in the grave, waiting for the promised resurrection of the dead.

The Gospel of the Kingdom of God

Jesus preached the gospel—the good news—of the coming Kingdom of God:

And it came to pass afterward, that he went throughout every city and village, preaching and shewing the glad tidings of the kingdom of God: and the twelve were with him (Luke 8:1)

Jesus prayed for the kingdom to come, and for the Father's will to be done here on earth:

Thy kingdom come. Thy will be done in earth, as it is in heaven (Matthew 6:10)

The Old Testament prophets described Jesus' return and His rule here on earth:

And he shall judge among the nations, and shall rebuke many people: and they shall beat their swords into plowshares, and their spears into pruninghooks: nation shall not lift up sword against nation, neither shall they learn war any more (Isaiah 2:4)

And his feet shall stand in that day upon the mount of Olives, which is before Jerusalem on the east, and the mount of Olives shall cleave in the midst thereof toward the east and toward the west . . . and the LORD my God shall come, and all the saints with thee (Zechariah 14:4,5).

What happens to those who receive eternal life at Jesus' return? Do they go to heaven forever? No. Those who receive eternal life at Jesus' return will be right here on earth with Jesus for 1000 years:

> **Blessed and holy is he that hath part in the first resurrection: on such the second death hath no power, but they shall be priests of God and of Christ, and shall reign with him a thousand years (Revelation 20:6)**

They will be here on earth with Jesus, teaching, governing, helping mankind. They will have a much more useful, meaningful and loving future than some sort of eternal vacation/party somewhere off in the clouds of heaven!

Jesus even told the twelve what they would be doing in His kingdom:

> **Ye are they which have continued with me in my temptations.**
>
> **And I appoint unto you a kingdom, as my Father hath appointed unto me;**
>
> **That ye may eat and drink at my table in my kingdom, and sit on thrones judging the twelve tribes of Israel (Luke 22:28-30)**

The apostle Paul preached about the kingdom of God:

> **And Paul dwelt two whole years in his own hired house, and received all that came in unto him,**
>
> **Preaching the kingdom of God, and teaching those things which concern the Lord Jesus Christ, with all confidence, no man forbidding him. (Acts 28:30,31)**

Here's Peter writing about the Kingdom of God:

Wherefore the rather, brethren, give diligence to make your calling and election sure: for if ye do these things, ye shall never fall:

For so an entrance shall be ministered unto you abundantly into the everlasting kingdom of our Lord and Saviour Jesus Christ (2 Peter 1:10,11)

The apostle James wrote:

Listen, my beloved brethren: Has God not chosen the poor of this world to be rich in faith and heirs of the kingdom which He promised to those who love Him? (James 2:5, NKJV)

The Old Testament prophet Daniel described the Kingdom of God taking the place of nations and kingdoms at the end time:

And in the days of these kings shall the God of heaven set up a kingdom, which shall never be destroyed: and the kingdom shall not be left to other people, but it shall break in pieces and consume all these kingdoms, and it shall stand for ever (Daniel 2:44)

The apostle John gave this description:

And the seventh angel sounded; and there were great voices in heaven, saying, The kingdoms of this world are become the kingdoms of our Lord, and of his Christ; and he shall reign for ever and ever (Revelation 11:15)

Here is another prophecy from Daniel about Jesus and the kingdom:

And there was given him dominion, and glory,

and a kingdom, that all people, nations, and languages, should serve him: his dominion is an everlasting dominion, which shall not pass away, and his kingdom that which shall not be destroyed (Daniel 7:14)

Here are more prophecies from the Old Testament prophets Jeremiah, Isaiah, Daniel, Zechariah and Micah:

> But with righteousness shall he judge the poor, and reprove with equity for the meek of the earth: and he shall smite the earth with the rod of his mouth, and with the breath of his lips shall he slay the wicked (Isaiah 11:1-4)

> And the kingdom and dominion, and the greatness of the kingdom under the whole heaven, shall be given to the people of the saints of the most High, whose kingdom is an everlasting kingdom, and all dominions shall serve and obey him (Daniel 7:27)

> And the LORD shall be king over all the earth: in that day shall there be one LORD, and his name one (Zechariah 14:9)

> They shall not hurt nor destroy in all my holy mountain: for the earth shall be full of the knowledge of the LORD, as the waters cover the sea (Isaiah 11:9)

> And they shall teach no more every man his neighbour, and every man his brother, saying, Know the LORD: for they shall all know me, from the least of them unto the greatest of them, saith the LORD (Jeremiah 31:34)

> But they shall sit every man under his vine and under his fig tree; and none shall make them afraid: for the mouth of the LORD of hosts hath spoken it. (Micah 4:4)

The End of Evil

During the 1000 years Satan will be isolated, prevented from influencing mankind. Satan will be confined: figuratively "chained" in a "bottomless pit" at the beginning of the 1000 years:

> And I saw an angel come down from heaven, having the key of the bottomless pit and a great chain in his hand.
>
> And he laid hold on the dragon, that old serpent, which is the Devil, and Satan, and bound him a thousand years,
>
> And cast him into the bottomless pit, and shut him up, and set a seal upon him, that he should deceive the nations no more, till the thousand years should be fulfilled: and after that he must be loosed a little season (Revelation 20:1-3)

Satan will be released, temporarily, at the end of the 1000 years:

> And when the thousand years are expired, Satan shall be loosed out of his prison,
>
> And shall go out to deceive the nations which are in the four quarters of the earth, Gog and Magog, to gather them together to battle: the number of whom is as the sand of the sea.

> And they went up on the breadth of the earth, and compassed the camp of the saints about, and the beloved city [referring to Jerusalem]: and fire came down from God out of heaven, and devoured them (Revelation 20:7-9)

Why is Satan released? Satan's release serves a purpose; Satan's release apparently serves as a time of judgment. Those alive at that time will need to sort out who and what to believe. When that purpose has been accomplished, Satan and his followers will be destroyed. Here's a description of Satan and his destruction:

> Thine heart was lifted up because of thy beauty, thou hast corrupted thy wisdom by reason of thy brightness: I will cast thee to the ground, I will lay thee before kings, that they may behold thee.
>
> Thou hast defiled thy sanctuaries by the multitude of thine iniquities, by the iniquity of thy traffick; therefore will I bring forth a fire from the midst of thee, it shall devour thee, and I will bring thee to ashes upon the earth in the sight of all them that behold thee.
>
> All they that know thee among the people shall be astonished at thee: thou shalt be a terror, and never shalt thou be any more (Ezekiel 28:17-19)

That's right: Satan will be destroyed, never to "be" anymore. So, how is it possible for Satan—a spirit being—to be made visible and to then be "devoured" by fire and reduced to ashes? There is only one explanation: Satan will be made mortal. Is it possible for a spirit being to be made mortal? Of course it is. For example, Jesus was the "Word" before He was made flesh:

> **In the beginning was the Word, and the Word was with God, and the Word was God.**
>
> **The same was in the beginning with God.**
>
> **All things were made by him; and without him was not any thing made that was made (John 1:1-3)**
>
> **And the Word was made flesh, and dwelt among us, (and we beheld his glory, the glory as of the only begotten of the Father,) full of grace and truth (John 1:14)**

Jesus died. He was really dead. Later, He said so:

> **I am he that liveth, and was dead; and, behold, I am alive for evermore, Amen; and have the keys of hell and of death (Revelation 1:18)**

For Jesus, there was a resurrection to immortality. For Satan, there will be no resurrection. There will be no hope of life. Satan's death will be the end of him: "never shalt thou be any more."

Those that joined Satan's rebellion will also be reduced to ashes:

> **For, behold, the day cometh, that shall burn as an oven; and all the proud, yea, and all that do wickedly, shall be stubble: and the day that cometh shall burn them up, saith the LORD of hosts, that it shall leave them neither root nor branch . . .**
>
> **And ye shall tread down the wicked; for they**

shall be ashes under the soles of your feet in the day that I shall do this, saith the LORD of hosts (Malachi 4:1,3)

We saw earlier that there will be a resurrection of "the rest of the dead" after the 1000 years:

But the rest of the dead lived not again until the thousand years were finished . . . (Revelation 20:5)

And I saw the dead, small and great, stand before God; and the books were opened: and another book was opened, which is the book of life: and the dead were judged out of those things which were written in the books, according to their works.

And the sea gave up the dead which were in it; and death and hell [hades, the grave] delivered up the dead which were in them: and they were judged every man according to their works (Revelation 20:12,13)

It is not clear whether this resurrection occurs before, or after, Satan leads his final rebellion. If it is before Satan's final rebellion, then that rebellion could serve as a time of judgment for those in this final resurrection as well as for those alive at that time.

The Fates

Continuing in Revelation 20:

And death and hell were cast into the lake of fire. This is the second death.

> **And whosoever was not found written in the book of life was cast into the lake of fire (Revelation 20:14,15)**

Those not found in the "book of life" will be "cast into the lake of fire." Being cast into the "lake of fire" *is* "the second death": death after judgment. Here's Revelation 21:8:

> **But the fearful, and unbelieving, and the abominable, and murderers, and whoremongers, and sorcerers, and idolaters, and all liars, shall have their part in the lake which burneth with fire and brimstone: which is the second death (Revelation 21:8)**

For those in the second death, there is no more hope of resurrection or life. It is the end of them. They are destroyed. Being "cast into the lake of fire" figuratively portrays their finished, permanent destruction.

The same applies to death and to hell ("hell" meaning hades, the grave). "And death and hell were cast into the lake of fire . . ." After the final judgment and the destruction of the wicked through death, death itself will be destroyed, never to happen again: everyone left will have received the gift of eternal life. As Paul wrote,

> **The last enemy that shall be destroyed is death (1 Corinthians 15:26)**

Death itself will be destroyed after the wicked have been destroyed through death. Likewise for "hell," the grave. "Hell" in Revelation 20:14 is from the Greek word ἄδης (hades) the place of the dead, the grave. Everyone will have been resurrected from the grave for judgment. No one will be left in the grave awaiting judgment. Therefore "hell"—the grave—will not exist or happen any more; it will have been destroyed, figuratively "cast into the lake of fire."

Jesus used "hell fire" to picture or illustrate the same destruction. He likened the fate of the wicked to being thrown into "hell fire." "Hell" in those verses is from the Greek γέεννα (geenna or gehenna): a reference to the dump outside Jerusalem. Everything thrown into that dump was permanently destroyed by fire and worms or maggots. More about that later.

At judgment some will see that others had received eternal life. They will realize that they, too, could have received eternal life were it not for their own foolish choices. Then there will be mental anguish, the "wailing" and "weeping and gnashing of teeth" that Jesus spoke of.

The New Earth and the New Heaven

After the judgment all the wicked will have been destroyed. Only those who had received eternal life will remain. Given that death and the grave had been destroyed, it is apparent that there will be no more mortals. Then what?

The universe will be re-created, made new:

And I saw a new heaven and a new earth: for the first heaven and the first earth were passed away; and there was no more sea.

And I John saw the holy city, new Jerusalem, coming down from God out of heaven, prepared

as a bride adorned for her husband.

And I heard a great voice out of heaven saying, Behold, the tabernacle of God is with men, and he will dwell with them, and they shall be his people, and God himself shall be with them, and be their God.

And God shall wipe away all tears from their eyes; and there shall be no more death, neither sorrow, nor crying, neither shall there be any more pain: for the former things are passed away.

And he that sat upon the throne said, Behold, I make all things new. And he said unto me, Write: for these words are true and faithful (Revelation 21:1-5)

Amazing. Incredible. God will come and dwell with us. There will be no more death, no more pain, no more tears, no more sorrow, no more crying. All things will be made new. We will inherit a new earth. That inheritance was spoken of by David in the Old Testament and in the New Testament, by Jesus:

But the meek shall inherit the earth; and shall delight themselves in the abundance of peace (Psalm 37:11)

Blessed are the meek: for they shall inherit the earth (Matthew 5:5)

Will there be no more literal, physical oceans or seas? Not necessarily. "Sea" and "waters" are used figuratively in prophecy, to represent people who do not know God. Here's an example, describing a worldly kingdom or "beast" rising up out of the "sea":

> And I stood upon the sand of the sea, and saw a beast rise up out of the sea, having seven heads and ten horns, and upon his horns ten crowns, and upon his heads the name of blasphemy (Revelation 13:1)

"Waters" is used in the same manner. In Revelation 17 we see a symbolic "great whore that sitteth upon many waters." The "whore" is false religion:

> And there came one of the seven angels which had the seven vials, and talked with me, saying unto me, Come hither; I will shew unto thee the judgment of the great whore that sitteth upon many waters:
>
> With whom the kings of the earth have committed fornication, and the inhabitants of the earth have been made drunk with the wine of her fornication (Revelation 17:1,2)

A few verses later we have this explanation:

> And he saith unto me, The waters which thou sawest, where the whore sitteth, are peoples, and multitudes, and nations, and tongues (Revelation 17:15)

In the new earth, there will be no more "sea," no more "multitudes, and nations" living apart from God.

The idea that we "go to heaven" and live there forever while the physical universe as we know goes on is not found in the Bible. We will live forever, yes, and God will come and dwell with us in His new creation. It is easy to get the wrong idea—that we go to heaven—when reading verses like this:

> **Rejoice, and be exceeding glad: for great is your reward in heaven: for so persecuted they the prophets which were before you (Matthew 5:12)**

Our reward is in heaven, kept there until Jesus returns and brings it to us:

> **And, behold, I come quickly; and my reward is with me, to give every man according as his work shall be (Revelation 22:12)**

When He comes, He will resurrect the just and give them their reward:

> **But when thou makest a feast, call the poor, the maimed, the lame, the blind:**
>
> **And thou shalt be blessed; for they cannot recompense thee: for thou shalt be recompensed at the resurrection of the just (Jesus, in Luke 14:13,14)**

We will be spirit beings, not mortal. As mortals we can hardly appreciate or comprehend what our new, spirit life will be like. We can only glimpse it as revealed to us by the holy spirit. Paul wrote:

> **But as it is written, Eye hath not seen, nor ear heard, neither have entered into the heart of man, the things which God hath prepared for them that love him.**
>
> **But God hath revealed them unto us by his Spirit: for the Spirit searcheth all things, yea, the deep things of God (1 Corinthians 2:9,10)**

Part 3: Other Doctrines

The Soul and Hell

Will the unsaved suffer eternal, conscious torment in a fiery hell? No; we have seen that the unsaved will die a "second death" after judgment:

But the fearful, and unbelieving, and the abominable, and murderers, and whoremongers, and sorcerers, and idolaters, and all liars, shall have their part in the lake which burneth with fire and brimstone: which is the second death (Revelation 21:8)

Does this "second death" refer to a second mortal death, but not to the death of the soul? If we have immortal souls will we always be conscious—somehow, someplace—even after a second mortal death? To understand the fate of the unsaved, we need to understand the real meaning of "hell." We also need to understand the "soul." We'll start with the soul.

Do we have immortal souls? Here's what Jesus had to say:

And fear not them which kill the body, but are not able to kill the soul: but rather fear him which is able to destroy both soul and body in hell (Matthew 10:28)

Really? Our soul can be destroyed? Did Jesus really mean "destroy"? The Greek word for "destroy" in this verse was ἀπόλλυμι (transliterated into English as "apollymi"). *Strong's Exhaustive Concordance of The Bible* provides the following definition for ἀπόλλυμι, (Strong's word # G622):

ἀπόλλυμι *apóllymi, ap-ol'-loo-mee; from G575 and*

the base of G3639; to destroy fully (reflexively, to perish, or lose), literally or figuratively:—destroy, die, lose, mar, perish.

You can easily look this up yourself with online tools or with resources such as *Strong's Exhaustive Concordance of the Bible*.

The "soul" can die:

The soul that sinneth, it shall die. The son shall not bear the iniquity of the father, neither shall the father bear the iniquity of the son: the righteousness of the righteous shall be upon him, and the wickedness of the wicked shall be upon him (Ezekiel 18:20)

So, how can we explain souls being destroyed? How can a soul die? It's simple, actually: the Biblical "soul" is not the same as the "immortal soul" which has come down to us from pagan Greek philosophy. "Soul" has two completely different definitions.

Try finding "immortal soul" in your Bible. It's not there. I searched many Bibles, including all these, and "immortal soul" was not in any of them:
- KJV (King James Version)
- NKJV (New King James Version)
- NET (New English Translation)
- NLT (New Living Translation)
- NIV (New International Version)
- ESV (English Standard Version)
- CSB (Christian Standard Bible)
- NASV (New American Standard Bible)
- RSV (Revised Standard Version)

ASV (American Standard Version)
YLT (Young's Literal Translation)
DBY (Darby Translation)
WEB (Webster's Bible)
HNV (Hebrew Names Version)
CEB (Common English Bible)
RHE (Douay-Rheims Catholic Bible)
GW (GOD'S WORD Translation)
GNT (Good News Translation)
CSB (Holman Christian Standard Bible)
LEB (Lexham English Bible)
NCV (New Century Version)
NIRV (New International Reader's Version)
NRS (New Revised Standard)
OJB (Orthodox Jewish Bible)
BBE (The Bible in Basic English)
CJB (The Complete Jewish Bible)
MSG (The Message Bible)
TMB (Third Millennium Bible)
TYN (Tyndale)
WNT (Weymouth New Testament)
WEB (World English Bible)
WYC (Wycliffe)

So, what is the "soul" in the Bible? It is not some sort of immortal component we have that leaves us when we die; that's a pagan idea promoted by Plato and other Greek philosophers hundreds of years before Christ. Consider what Plato wrote about 360 BC:

"Do we believe that there is such a thing as death? And is this anything but the separation of soul and body? And being dead is the attainment of this separation;

when the soul exists in herself, and is parted from the body and the body is parted from the soul . . . is not the conclusion of the whole matter this? - that the soul is in the very likeness of the divine, and immortal, and intelligible, and uniform, and indissoluble, and unchangeable; and the body is in the very likeness of the human, and mortal, and unintelligible, and multiform, and dissoluble, and changeable . . . beyond question the soul is immortal and imperishable, and our souls will truly exist in another world!" (Plato, in *Phaedo*, about 360 BC)

How did the "immortal soul" enter traditional Christian doctrine? It came quite naturally in the early church as people converted from their pagan Greek roots. Trouble is, they did not leave all their roots behind. Today the "immortal soul" that will always live on—someplace, somehow—has become firmly embedded into traditional Christian doctrine. Here is a quote from evangelist Billy Graham, teaching everyone's soul will always live somewhere forever:

But you cannot change the fact that you're a living soul, and that you're going to live somewhere forever. That's a sobering thought . . . That's the part of you that will be living a thousand years from now, either in heaven or hell. (Billy Graham, campaign sermon, Washington, DC)

Matthew 10:28 is by no means the only verse about ἀπόλλυμι — being fully destroyed or perishing. Here's John 3:16, a verse almost every Christian knows:

For God so loved the world, that he gave his only begotten Son, that whosoever believeth in him should not perish, but have everlasting life.

"Perish" in that verse is from the very same Greek word ἀπόλλυμι. We will either perish, fully destroyed, or else we will have eternal life. Salvation is not about **where** you will spend eternity. Salvation is about whether you will even **have** an eternity!

Here's another verse about perishing:

The Lord is not slack concerning his promise, as some men count slackness; but is longsuffering to us-ward, not willing that any should perish, but that all should come to repentance (2 Peter 3:9)

"Perish" is from the same Greek word ἀπόλλυμι. If we'll "come to repentance" we can avoid perishing, we can avoid destruction.

Jesus gave a similar warning in Luke 13:4,5:

Or those eighteen, upon whom the tower in Siloam fell, and slew them, think ye that they were sinners above all men that dwelt in Jerusalem?

I tell you, Nay: but, except ye repent, ye shall all likewise perish.

Again, "perish" is the same Greek word ἀπόλλυμι.

Jesus said:

Enter ye in at the strait gate: for wide is the gate, and broad is the way, that leadeth to destruction, and many there be which go in thereat:

Because strait is the gate, and narrow is the way, which leadeth unto life, and few there be that find it (Matthew 7:13,14)

"Destruction" in the first verse is from the Greek

ἀπώλεια, a different form of ἀπόλλυμι. Strong's gives this definition:

ἀπώλεια apóleia, ap-o'-li-a; from a presumed derivative of G622; ruin or loss (physical, spiritual or eternal):—damnable(-nation), destruction, die, perdition, X perish, pernicious ways, waste.

As we saw in John 3:16, the alternatives are not life in one place or another. No, the alternatives are either to perish, or to live. The life or perish alternatives are very clear in John 10:27,28:

My sheep hear my voice, and I know them, and they follow me:

And I give unto them eternal life; and they shall never perish, neither shall any man pluck them out of my hand.

"Perish," again, is from ἀπόλλυμι. And note this: eternal life is a gift. The next verse makes this clear:

For the wages of sin is death; but the gift of God is eternal life through Jesus Christ our Lord (Romans 6:23)

Eternal life is a gift from God. Common sense: we would have no need to receive eternal life as a gift if we already had an immortal soul.

Salvation is not about *where* you'll spend eternity. You won't even *have* an eternity—of any sort, anywhere—unless you receive the gift of eternal life! Without the gift of eternal life, you will perish.

We've looked at New Testament verses about perishing and destruction. Now here are a few verses from the Old

Testament. The wicked will be destroyed: they will perish and not "be" anymore:

> For yet a little while, and the wicked shall not be: yea, thou shalt diligently consider his place, and it shall not be (Psalms 37:10)
>
> When the wicked spring as the grass, and when all the workers of iniquity do flourish; it is that they shall be destroyed for ever (Psalms 92:7)
>
> The way of the LORD is strength to the upright: but destruction shall be to the workers of iniquity (Proverbs 10:29)
>
> As the whirlwind passeth, so is the wicked no more: but the righteous is an everlasting foundadation (Proverbs 10:25)
>
> Knowest thou not this of old, since man was placed upon earth,
>
> That the triumphing of the wicked is short, and the joy of the hypocrite but for a moment?
>
> Though his excellency mount up to the heavens, and his head reach unto the clouds;
>
> Yet he shall perish for ever like his own dung: they which have seen him shall say, Where is he? (Job 20:4-7)

"Soul" in the Bible has a different definition than Plato's immortal soul. The Biblical "soul" is not immortal: it can perish, it can be destroyed and not "be" any more.

Genesis 2:7 gives us an insight into the meaning of "soul" in the Bible:

And the LORD God formed man of the dust of the ground, and breathed into his nostrils the breath of life; and man became a living soul (Genesis 2:7)

The man was not *given* a soul. The man *became* a soul. The man became a soul, a living being, when he received the breath of life from God. "Soul" in that verse is from the Hebrew word נפש ("nephesh") which means a living creature, a live animal. The very same Hebrew word is used for "the moving creature that hath life" (Genesis 1:20), the "living creature that moveth" (Genesis 1:21), the "living creature" (Genesis 1:24), the "thing that creepeth upon the earth, wherein there is life" (Genesis 1:30) and the "living creature" (Genesis 2:19).

"Soul" in the Bible does not mean some sort of immortal spiritual component which floats out of your body when you die. We don't *have* souls: we *are* souls—but with a different definition: we are living beings, persons or selves with consciousness, thoughts, emotions, character, hopes etc.

Biblical context shows "soul" refers to a person or persons, or to the self as in "I am," or to one's own life or existence. Here are three New Testament examples:

Referring to persons or people:

And we were in all in the ship two hundred threescore and sixteen souls (Paul, in Acts 27:37)

Referring to one's self, as in "I am . . . ":

Then saith he unto them, My soul is exceeding sorrowful, even unto death: tarry ye here, and watch with me (Jesus, in Matthew 26:38)

Referring to a person's life or existence:

For what is a man profited, if he shall gain the whole world, and lose his own soul? Or what shall a man give in exchange for his soul (Matthew 16:26)

Why were the first couple removed from the garden? To prevent them from eating of the tree of life and then living forever. Conclusion: they did not have immortality or immortal souls:

And the LORD God said, Behold, the man is become as one of us, to know good and evil: and now, lest he put forth his hand, and take also of the tree of life, and eat, and live for ever:

Therefore the LORD God sent him forth from the garden of Eden, to till the ground from whence he was taken (Genesis 3:22,23)

The "immortal soul" that floats out of you when you die is a myth passed down from pagan religion and adopted into mainstream Christianity over the centuries. Take away the "immortal soul" error, and immediately there is no more need to try to "explain" where the immortal soul goes—or what it does—for eternity. Unsaved persons—souls—will simply perish via the "second death" after judgment. Everyone else will receive the gift of eternal life and never perish.

The Spirit: the Breath of Life

Man became a living soul, a living being, when he received "the breath of life"—though his nostrils—from

God:

> And the LORD God formed man of the dust of the ground, and breathed into his nostrils the breath of life; and man became a living soul (Genesis 2:7)

When we die this "breath of life" leaves us. We stop breathing. Notice the following verses; the breath of life is the "spirit" of God:

> All the while my breath is in me, and the spirit of God is in my nostrils (Job 27:3)

> Then shall the dust return to the earth as it was: and the spirit shall return unto God who gave it (Ecclesiastes 12:7, describing death)

> His breath goeth forth, he returneth to his earth; in that very day his thoughts perish (Psalm 146:4)

At death we exhale for the last time. Our "thoughts perish": our consciousness stops. We return to the earth, the grave.

The body without the "spirit," the breath of life, is dead:

> For as the body without the spirit is dead, so faith without works is dead also (James 2:26)

"Spirit" in James 2:26 is from the Greek word πνεῦμα ("pneuma") defined (in *Strong's Definitions*) as: "a current of air, i.e. breath (blast) or a breeze." Today we have *pneu*matic—air powered—tools.

> And they stoned Stephen, calling upon God, and saying, Lord Jesus, receive my spirit (Acts 7:59)

"Spirit" is from the same Greek word πνεῦμα "pneuma." Stephen was calling on the Lord to receive back the breath of life, not some sort of immortal soul.

> **And after three days and an half the Spirit of life from God entered into them, and they stood upon their feet; and great fear fell upon them which saw them (Revelation 11:11, describing the resurrection of the future "two witnesses.")**

"Spirit" is from the same Greek word πνεῦμα "pneuma." The breath or air of life would come back to the two witnesses.

> **And when Jesus had cried out with a loud voice, He said, "Father, 'into Your hands I commit My spirit.'" Having said this, He breathed His last (Luke 23:46, NKJV; NIV and RSV are similar)**

"Spirit" in this verse is from the same Greek word πνεῦμα "pneuma." "Breathed his last" is from the Greek word ἐκπνέω ("ekpneo"). It's the Greek words ἐκ and πνέω assembled into one new word. "Ek" means out, "pneo" means blow or breathe. Jesus breathed out his last breath and died.

Regrettably the KJV uses "gave up the ghost" instead of "breathed his last" in that verse (and in Mark 15:37 and 39):

> **And when Jesus had cried with a loud voice, he said, Father, into thy hands I commend my spirit: and having said thus, he gave up the ghost (Luke 23:46, KJV)**

"Ghost" misleads many into wrong conclusions, for example, that Jesus was letting go of an immortal soul.

Most other common Bibles render ἐκπνέω as "breathed His last" rather than "gave up the ghost." Here's a couple more examples:

> Then Jesus, calling out with a loud voice, said, "Father, into your hands I commit my spirit!" And having said this he breathed his last (Luke 23:46, ESV)
>
> Then Jesus, calling out with a loud voice, said, "Father, into your hands I commit my spirit!" And after he said this he breathed his last (Luke 23:46, NET)

The "soul"—correctly understood—is the self, the person, the life; it is not some kind of immortal spiritual thing that floats out of the body at death. And soul should not be confused with the πνεῦμα "spirit," the breath that gives life to the body.

The Meanings of "Hell"

We have solid evidence that the unsaved will be destroyed; they will not even "be" any more. So, what is "hell" in the Bible? If "hell" is not eternal conscious torment, and not eternal conscious separation, then what is it?

Using an online search tool we can easily search the KJV and find all the verses where "hell" appears. We can also look up what word was used in the Hebrew and Greek texts from which the Bible was translated.

"Hell" in the King James Version of the Bible (KJV) comes from several different Hebrew and Greek words, with different meanings. Later Bibles, as we'll see, dropped this generic use of "hell" and used words better reflecting the original Greek words. Some Bibles do not even use "hell"!

In the King James Version of the Bible "hell" appears 54 times: 31 times in the Old Testament and 23 times in the New Testament.

In all 31 Old Testament instances, "hell" is from the Hebrew word שאול transliterated as *she'ol* or *Sheol* in English. But note this: that same Hebrew word is also translated in other ways; it is not always translated as "hell." In another 31 other instances it is translated as "grave" and in three more instances it is translated as "pit."

"Hell" in the Old Testament essentially means "the place of the dead": the pit, the grave, the tomb.

In the New Testament (KJV) "hell" appears 23 times, but does not come from just one Greek word. "Hell" in the KJV NT comes from three different Greek words, each of which has a different meaning. The three Greek words are:

• ἅδης ("hades"), a noun; Strong's G86; 10 times

• γέεννα ("geenna" or "gehenna"), a noun: Strong's G1067; 12 times

• ταρταρωσας a verb, an inflection or variant of the Greek ταρταρόω; transliterated ("tartaroo"); Strong's G5020; used only once.

The first of these, ἅδης or "hades," is much like the Hebrew שאול "Sheol," referring to the grave, the place of the dead. In one instance in the KJV, it was actually correctly translated "grave" rather than "hell":

> **O death, where is thy sting? O grave, where is thy victory? (1Corinthians 15:55)**

Let's compare some Bibles. Let's look at some of the verses where the KJV says "hell" and see how some other Bibles render same verse.

There are ten verses where the Greek ἅδης (hades, the grave, the place of the dead) was translated as "hell" in the King James Version, New Testament. The next two pages examine four of those ten verses. The KJV and thirteen other Bibles are listed just below each verse. In that list you'll see how each of those other thirteen Bibles rendered ἅδης in that same verse: usually as "Hades," sometimes as "She'ol" (referencing the Hebrew word) or as "the grave" or as "among the dead" or as "the realm of the dead"—but not as "hell."

He seeing this before spake of the resurrection of Christ, that his soul was not left in hell, neither his flesh did see corruption (Acts 2:31, KJV)

KJV: hell	ESV: Hades
NKJV: Hades	YLT: hades
NET: Hades	CSB: Hades
NLT: among the dead	DBY: hades
NIV: realm of the dead	HNV: She'ol
RSV: Hades	NASB: HADES
ASV: Hades	TS2009: She'ol

I am he that liveth, and was dead; and, behold, I am alive for evermore, Amen; and have the keys of hell and of death (Revelation 1:18, KJV)

KJV: hell	ESV: Hades
NKJV: Hades	YLT: hades
Net: Hades	CSB: Hades
NLT: the grave	DBY: hades
NIV: Hades	HNV: She'ol
RSV: Hades	NASB: HADES
ASV: Hades	TS2009: She'ol

And the sea gave up the dead which were in it; and death and hell delivered up the dead which were in them: and they were judged every man according to their works (Revelation 20:13, KJV)

    KJV: hell   ESV: Hades

    NKJV: Hades   YLT: hades

    Net: Hades   CSB: Hades

    NLT: the grave*   DBY: hades

    NIV: Hades   HNV: She'ol

    RSV: Hades   NASB: HADES

    ASV: Hades   TS2009: She'ol

    * footnoted: Greek *and Hades*

And death and hell were cast into the lake of fire. This is the second death (Revelation 20:14, KJV)

    KJV: hell   ESV: Hades

    NKJV: Hades   YLT: hades

    NET: Hades   CSB: Hades

    NLT: the grave*   DBY: hades

    NIV: Hades   HNV: She'ol

    RSV: Hades   NASB: HADES

    ASV: Hades   TS2009: She'ol

    * footnoted: Greek *and Hades*

Next, some examples where "hell" came from γέεννα or "gehenna." This would be a good time to point out that fire is never mentioned in the ten "hell" verses using the Greek ἄδης or "hades." However, for the twelve "hell" verses from the Greek γέεννα or "gehenna," fire is often mentioned, and there is good reason for that. Here is a definition of γέεννα or "gehenna" from Easton's *Illustrated Bible Dictionary*:

> *Gehenna (originally Ge bene Hinnom; I.e., "the valley of the sons of Hinnom"), a deep, narrow glen to the south of Jerusalem, where the idolatrous Jews offered their children in sacrifice to Molech (2 Chronicles 28:3 ; 33:6 ; Jeremiah 7:31 ; 19:2-6). This valley afterwards became the common receptacle for all the refuse of the city. Here the dead bodies of animals and of criminals, and all kinds of filth, were cast and consumed by fire kept always burning. It thus in process of time became the image of the place of everlasting destruction. In this sense it is used by our Lord in Matthew 5:22 Matthew 5:29 Matthew 5:30 ; 10:28 ; 18:9 ; Matthew 23:15 Matthew 23:33 ; Mark 9:43 Mark 9:45 Mark 9:47 ; Luke 12:5 . In these passages, and also in James 3:6 , the word is uniformly rendered "hell," the Revised Version placing "Gehenna" in the margin.* (M.G. Easton M.A., D.D., *Illustrated Bible Dictionary, Third Edition*, published by Thomas Nelson, 1897. Public Domain)

"Gehenna" in Jesus' time was the dump on the south side of Jerusalem, where constant fire and maggots destroyed whatever refuse was thrown in. Jesus likened the fate of the unsaved to being thrown into the gehenna dump, into "gehenna fire." Figuratively thrown into the "dump," they would be permanently destroyed. This permanent destruction is the same ἀπόλλυμι—perishing, destruction—we have seen in Matthew 10:28, John 3:16, Luke 13:5, John 10:28 and 2 Peter 3:9. It is the same destruction and no longer "being" we saw in Old Testament verses. It is the same destruction as being cast into "the lake of fire, which is the second death" as we saw in Revelation 21:8.

Here are four of the twelve verses where "hell" in the KJV NT comes from the Greek γέεννα. In the original Greek some verses include a direct reference to fire, alluding to the fire in the γέεννα dump. Where they do, the entire expression about hell and fire is shown next to the other Bibles listed. Note: in some Bibles, including *Young's Literal Translation* (YLT), "hell" is never used.

And fear not them which kill the body, but are not able to kill the soul: but rather fear him which is able to destroy both soul and body in hell (Matthew 10:28, KJV)

KJV: hell	ESV: hell*
NKJV: hell	YLT: gehenna
NET: hell	CSB: hell
NLT: hell*	DBY: hell
NIV: hell	HNV: Gehinnom
RSV: hell	NASB: hell**
ASV: hell	TS2009: GěHinnom

footnoted:

* Greek *Gehenna*

** GR Gehenna

But I say unto you, That whosoever is angry with his brother without a cause shall be in danger of the judgment: and whosoever shall say to his brother, Raca, shall be in danger of the council: but whosoever shall say, Thou fool, shall be in danger of hell fire (Jesus, in Matthew 5:22, KJV)

    KJV: hell fire

    NKJV: hell fire

    NET: to fiery hell

    NLT: the fires of hell*

    NIV: the fire of hell

    RSV: the hell of fire

    ASV: the hell of fire

    ESV: the hell of fire*

    YLT: the gehenna of the fire

    CSB: hellfire**

    DBY: the hell of fire

    HNV: the fire of Gehinnom

    NASB: the fiery hell***

    TS2009: fire of GěHinnom

        footnoted:

* Greek *Gehenna*

** Lit *the gehenna of fire*

*** Literally: *Gehenna of fire*

And if thine eye offend thee, pluck it out, and cast it from thee: it is better for thee to enter into life with one eye, rather than having two eyes to be cast into hell fire (Matthew 18:9, KJV)

    KJV: hell fire

    NKJV: hell fire

    NET: into fiery hell

    NLT: the fire of hell*

    NIV: the fire of hell

    RSV: the hell of fire

    ASV: the hell of fire

    ESV: the hell of fire**

    YLT: the gehenna of the fire

    CSB: hellfire***

    DBY: the hell of fire

    HNV: the Gehinnom of fire

    NASB: the fiery hell****

    TS2009: fire of GěHinnom

        footnoted:

* Greek *the gehenna of fire*

** Greek *Gehenna*

*** Lit *gehenna of fire*

**** Literally: *Gehenna of fire*

But I will forewarn you whom ye shall fear: Fear him, which after he hath killed hath power to cast into hell; yea, I say unto you, Fear him (Luke 12:5, KJV)

KJV: hell	ESV: hell*
NKJV: hell	YLT: gehenna
NET: hell	CSB: hell
NLT: hell*	DBY: hell
NIV: hell	HNV: Gehinnom
RSV: hell	NASB: hell**
ASV: hell	TS2009: GĕHinnom

footnoted:

* Greek *Gehenna*

** Gr *Gehenna*

The third Greek word translated as "hell" in the KJV NT regards fallen angels rather than men, and has nothing to do with the grave or with destruction. This third Greek word is ταρταρωσας and appears in only one verse: 2 Peter 2:4. The Greek word ταρταρωσας is an inflection or variation of the base Greek word ταρταρόω ("tartaroo"), a verb, meaning to cast down or thrust down to the deepest pit. Peter used ταρταρωσας to figuratively illustrate the condition of some fallen angels. Those angels had been put into a place or condition of restraint or isolation and thus prevented from influencing or meddling with mankind. They are being held there in figurative "chains of darkness" awaiting judgment. Here is 2 Peter 2:4:

For if God spared not the angels that sinned, but cast them down to hell, and delivered them into chains of darkness, to be reserved unto judgment (2 Peter 2:4, KJV)

KJV: hell	ESV: hell*
NKJV: hell	YLT: Tartarus
NET: hell	CSB: hell*
NLT: hell*	DBY: pit of gloom
NIV: hell*	HNV: Tartarus
RSV: hell	NASB: hell
ASV: hell	TS2009: Tartaros**

footnoted:

* Greek *Tartarus*

** Possibly from Hebrew: Tahti

Jude verse 6 speaks of the same imprisonment:

And the angels which kept not their first estate, but left their own habitation, he hath reserved in everlasting chains under darkness unto the judgment of the great day (Jude, verse 6)

Previously we saw that Satan also will be imprisoned in a figurative "bottomless pit" or place of restraint for 1000 years after Jesus' return:

And I saw an angel come down from heaven, having the key of the bottomless pit and a great

> chain in his hand.
>
> And he laid hold on the dragon, that old serpent, which is the Devil, and Satan, and bound him a thousand years,
>
> And cast him into the bottomless pit, and shut him up, and set a seal upon him, that he should deceive the nations no more, till the thousand years should be fulfilled: and after that he must be loosed a little season (Revelation 20:1-3)

We have seen examples of the ten verses where "hell" in the KJV NT is from ἅδης "hades," the grave. We've seen examples of the twelve verses where "hell" is from γέεννα "gehenna," referring to the dump where refuse was thrown for permanent destruction. *Jesus illustrated the destruction of the unsaved by likening it to the permanent destruction of rubbish thrown into the dump outside Jerusalem.* And last, we've seen "hell" translated from ταρταρωσας, referring to angels being held in restraint until their judgment.

The unsaved have no existence after the "second death." They will be destroyed and not "be" any more. Does that mean no one suffers eternal conscious torment in some kind of fiery hell? Exactly!

Common sense: take away the "immortal soul" error and there is no longer any need to speculate "where" immortal souls of the unsaved "spend" eternity! *There will be no eternity—no eternal life anywhere—unless eternal life is received as a gift from God.*

What do you do with your trash? Do you take it out to your backyard and beat it with a stick, every day, day after day? I hope not. Aside being a waste of your time and effort, your neighbors would think you're crazy. What do you do? You throw it away; it goes to the dump for destruction.

That is similar to what will happen to the wicked. They will be destroyed. Both body and soul—the self, the life, the existence—can be destroyed. Jesus said:

And fear not them which kill the body, but are not able to kill the soul: but rather fear him which is able to destroy both soul and body in hell (Matthew 10:28)

Again, "hell" in that verse is from the Greek γέεννα "gehenna," the dump where trash was thrown for destruction. The unsaved will suffer a similar fate: permanent destruction.

This would be a good time to look at a verse that troubles many. Here Jesus describes the fate of the unsaved:

And these shall go away into everlasting punishment: but the righteous into life eternal. (Jesus, in Matthew 25:46)

When a criminal is executed, that punishment is complete, final and irreversible. It's permanent; it's done. It is not perpetual, ongoing punishing. The punishment of the unsaved will be "everlasting" in the same sense: it will be complete, final and irreversible . . . permanent and done. It will be the "second death," not perpetual, active, ongoing punishing.

The words "permanent" and "final" never appear in the KJV; "everlasting" is often used instead. It's a mistake to assume "everlasting" means an ongoing, perpetual process. It can refer to a permanent, finished, final and irreversible condition.

If you've been told that the unsaved are perpetually punished in some sort of fiery "hell" then you would, quite naturally, take that verse as confirmation of what you've been told. We hear and read and interpret through the "lens" of what we already think to be true.

Naturally, translation of scripture is done through the lens of what the translators already believe. The King James Version's unfortunate use of the word "hell" has steered many into belief in a hell where the unsaved suffer eternal, conscious torment. That idea, like the immortal soul idea, comes down to us from pagan mythology, not from the Bible. The Bible shows that the unsaved are destroyed, permanently, upon their "second death" after judgment.

Those who teach eternal, conscious torment in a fiery hell are damaging Christianity and insulting God. The idea that a merciful, loving God would mercilessly, hopelessly, endlessly (and *pointlessly*) torment a human being for ever is blatantly ridiculous. It paints God as a sadistic monster. I'm not sure why anyone would desire to live forever with such a monster.

It pains me to see preachers trying to convince their listeners that eternal torment is "justice." There is no way a short human life of rebellion against God deserves an endless eternity of pathetic torment. No, it's not "justice": it's **ridiculous**. And it makes Christianity look ridiculous. Can we stop the ignorance, please?

Born-Again

Christians often claim they have been "born again." Having been born again, they often presume they have "eternal security" simply because—by literal, physical analogy—a person can not be unborn or be returned to the womb. So they say "once born-again, always born-again."

It's not the analogy that's faulty. It's the assumption that they have been born again that's faulty. Let's look at Jesus' conversation with Nicodemus:

> **There was a man of the Pharisees, named Nicodemus, a ruler of the Jews: The same came to Jesus by night, and said unto him, Rabbi, we know that thou art a teacher come from God: for no man can do these miracles that thou doest, except God be with him.**
>
> **Jesus answered and said unto him, Verily, verily, I say unto thee, Except a man be born again, he cannot see the kingdom of God.**
>
> **Nicodemus saith unto him, How can a man be born when he is old? Can he enter the second time into his mother's womb, and be born?**
>
> **Jesus answered, Verily, verily, I say unto thee, Except a man be born of water and of the Spirit, he cannot enter into the kingdom of God.**
>
> **That which is born of the flesh is flesh; and that which is born of the Spirit is spirit.**
>
> **Marvel not that I said unto thee, Ye must be born again.**

The wind bloweth where it listeth, and thou hearest the sound thereof, but canst not tell whence it cometh, and whither it goeth: so is every one that is born of the Spirit (John 3:1-8)

We must be born again or born of the spirit to see or enter the kingdom of God. So what is it like to have been born of the spirit? Let's look again at Jesus' description:

The wind bloweth where it listeth, and thou hearest the sound thereof, but canst not tell whence it cometh, and whither it goeth: so is every one that is born of the Spirit (John 3:8)

No one today who claims to be "born again" fits *that* description. They can not move invisibly, like the wind. But Jesus could do that after His resurrection. He was able to move invisibly, and appear and disappear in front of His disciples. Jesus had not been resurrected as a mortal. He was raised with what the apostle Paul described as an immortal "spiritual body." He had been born again or born of the spirit. He was able to manifest or reveal Himself as physical and touchable, but was not mortal. Born of the flesh mortals can not disappear and reappear.

Jesus explained to Nicodemus,

That which is born of the flesh is flesh; and that which is born of the Spirit is spirit (John 3:6)

You can't be both at the same time; you're either flesh, or, you're spirit. They are two different things.

Jesus was the "firstfruits," the first to go from mortality to immortal life, from flesh to spirit. When He returns those who have died "in Christ" will be resurrected. Then, like Jesus, they too will have immortal, spiritual bodies.

They will have been born of the spirit. In a letter to the Colossians, the apostle Paul described Jesus:

> And he is the head of the body, the church: who is the beginning, the firstborn from the dead; that in all things he might have the preeminence (Colossians 1:18)

Paul wrote to the Corinthians:

> But every man in his own order: Christ the firstfruits; afterward they that are Christ's at his coming (1 Corinthians 15:23)

In a letter to the Philippians, the apostle Paul described the receipt of spiritual bodies at Jesus' return:

> For our conversation is in heaven; from whence also we look for the Saviour, the Lord Jesus Christ:
>
> Who shall change our vile body, that it may be fashioned like unto his glorious body, according to the working whereby he is able even to subdue all things unto himself (Philippians 3:20,21)

Paul wrote about the bodies of the elect at death and at resurrection. When we die our natural, mortal body is "sown" or planted back into the ground, the grave. At Jesus' return those who have died "in Christ" will be resurrected with an immortal, spiritual body:

> So also is the resurrection of the dead. It is sown in corruption; it is raised in incorruption:
>
> It is sown in dishonour; it is raised in glory: it is sown in weakness; it is raised in power:
>
> It is sown a natural body; it is raised a spiritual body. There is a natural body, and there is a

spiritual body (1 Corinthians 15:42-44)

We will not be born of the spirit until we receive a spiritual body, at the resurrection at His return. Meanwhile in this mortal life we are *begotten* of the spirit, if we have received the holy spirit. We can never be born of the spirit without first being begotten of the spirit. But being begotten of the spirit is by no means a guarantee we will later be born of the spirit. Even after being made a "partaker" of the holy spirit it is possible to "fall away" or abort by our own choice or neglect:

> **For it is impossible for those who were once enlightened, and have tasted of the heavenly gift, and were made partakers of the Holy Ghost,**
>
> **And have tasted the good word of God, and the powers of the world to come,**
>
> **If they shall fall away, to renew them again unto repentance; seeing they crucify to themselves the Son of God afresh, and put him to an open shame (Hebrews 6:4-6)**

Both Jesus and Paul explained we must be born of the spirit—we must have an immortal spiritual body—before we can enter or inherit the Kingdom of God. Here is Jesus, again, speaking to Nicodemus:

> **Jesus answered, Verily, verily, I say unto thee, Except a man be born of water and of the Spirit, he cannot enter into the kingdom of God (Jesus, in John 3:5)**

Paul said the same: as "flesh and blood" we can not inherit the kingdom of God: we must first receive an immortal, spiritual body, at Jesus' return at "the last trump":

> Now this I say, brethren, that flesh and blood cannot inherit the kingdom of God; neither doth corruption inherit incorruption.
>
> Behold, I shew you a mystery; We shall not all sleep, but we shall all be changed,
>
> In a moment, in the twinkling of an eye, at the last trump: for the trumpet shall sound, and the dead shall be raised incorruptible, and we shall be changed.
>
> For this corruptible must put on incorruption, and this mortal must put on immortality.
>
> So when this corruptible shall have put on incorruption, and this mortal shall have put on immortality, then shall be brought to pass the saying that is written, Death is swallowed up in victory (Paul, in 1 Corinthians 15:50-54)

Perhaps you're wondering, What does it mean to enter or inherit the kingdom of God?

There are many verses about inheriting or entering the kingdom of God. Here are a few:

> Fear not, little flock; for it is your Father's good pleasure to give you the kingdom (Luke 12:32)

Jesus described how He would reward the faithful upon His return:

> Then shall the King say unto them on his right hand, Come, ye blessed of my Father, inherit the kingdom prepared for you from the foundation of the world (Matthew 25:34)

Note that their inheritance of the kingdom was planed from the start, from the beginning of the world!)

As we've seen, those who receive spiritual bodies at the "first resurrection," at Jesus' return, will be immortal, so death will have no power over them. They will be with Jesus, ruling with Him here on Earth:

> **Blessed and holy is he that hath part in the first resurrection: on such the second death hath no power, but they shall be priests of God and of Christ, and shall reign with him a thousand years (Revelation 20:6)**

Revelation 5:9,10 speaks of Jesus from the elect's point of view, saying:

> **. . . thou wast slain, and hast redeemed us to God by thy blood out of every kindred, and tongue, and people, and nation; And hast made us unto our God kings and priests: and we shall reign on the earth. (Revelation 5:9,10)**

Before anyone can inherit the kingdom of God, they must first receive an immortal, spiritual body, like Jesus had after His resurrection. They will receive that body at the first resurrection, at Jesus' return. Then they will have been born again or born of the spirit. That's the real meaning of "born again."

Meanwhile in this mortal life we may be *begotten* of the spirit: we may have received the holy spirit.

The apostle John illustrated the difference between begotten and born. Upon receiving immortality at Jesus' return, we will have been born again, born of the spirit or born of God and will not sin. But during this mortal life—begotten of God—we are capable of sin; in repentance we are to keep ourselves from sin:

> **We know that whosoever is born of God sinneth not; but he that is begotten of God keepeth himself, and that wicked one toucheth him not (1 John 5:18)**

Lazarus and the Rich Man

The account of Lazarus and the rich man has probably caused more controversy and confusion than any other passage in the Bible. Let's take a look at it:

> **There was a certain rich man, which was clothed in purple and fine linen, and fared sumptuously every day:**
>
> **And there was a certain beggar named Lazarus, which was laid at his gate, full of sores,**
>
> **And desiring to be fed with the crumbs which fell from the rich man's table: moreover the dogs came and licked his sores.**
>
> **And it came to pass, that the beggar died, and was carried by the angels into Abraham's bosom: the rich man also died, and was buried;**
>
> **And in hell he lift up his eyes, being in torments, and seeth Abraham afar off, and Lazarus in his bosom.**
>
> **And he cried and said, Father Abraham, have mercy on me, and send Lazarus, that he may dip the tip of his finger in water, and cool my tongue; for I am tormented in this flame.**

> But Abraham said, Son, remember that thou in thy lifetime receivedst thy good things, and likewise Lazarus evil things: but now he is comforted, and thou art tormented.
>
> And beside all this, between us and you there is a great gulf fixed: so that they which would pass from hence to you cannot; neither can they pass to us, that would come from thence.
>
> Then he said, I pray thee therefore, father, that thou wouldest send him to my father's house:
>
> For I have five brethren; that he may testify unto them, lest they also come into this place of torment.
>
> Abraham saith unto him, They have Moses and the prophets; let them hear them.
>
> And he said, Nay, father Abraham: but if one went unto them from the dead, they will repent.
>
> And he said unto him, If they hear not Moses and the prophets, neither will they be persuaded, though one rose from the dead (Luke 16:19-31)

The account of Lazarus and the rich man is not a story, to be taken literally; it is a parable; it's symbolic. Jesus spoke to the people in parables:

> But without a parable spake he not unto them: and when they were alone, he expounded all things to his disciples (Mark 4:34)
>
> All these things spake Jesus unto the multitude in parables; and without a parable spake he not unto them (Matthew 13:34)

If taken as a literal story with Lazarus and the rich man being real people, then the account would conflict with scripture. There is no resurrection and no judgment in the account. But Jesus said there will be a resurrection and a judgment before anyone is condemned:

> **Marvel not at this: for the hour is coming, in the which all that are in the graves shall hear his voice,**
>
> **And shall come forth; they that have done good, unto the resurrection of life; and they that have done evil, unto the resurrection of damnation (John 5:28,29)**

The resurrection for judgment will be in the future; there is no literal "rich man" now in "torments." And neither Abraham nor Lazarus are in heaven. Jesus said so:

> **And no man hath ascended up to heaven, but he that came down from heaven, even the Son of man which is in heaven (Jesus, in John 3:13)**

That's right: Abraham, Moses, Elijah, David and all the others are still in their graves, waiting for their resurrection. The apostle Peter confirmed that even David, a man after God's own heart, was still in his tomb and had not ascended to heaven:

> **Men and brethren, let me freely speak unto you of the patriarch David, that he is both dead and buried, and his sepulchre is with us unto this day . . .**
>
> **For David is not ascended into the heavens: but he saith himself, The LORD said unto my Lord, Sit thou on my right hand, Until I make thy foes**

thy footstool (Acts 2:29,34,35)

So, what does the parable mean? Jesus gave a hint to the identity of the rich man: He said the rich man had five brothers. The Jews knew their genealogy well and realized the rich man symbolized them, the Jews: the ancestral father of their tribe, a man named Judah, had five brothers. These six were the sons of Jacob and Leah. (Jacob fathered another six sons—half-brothers to Judah—by other women. The twelve sons became the ancestral fathers of the "twelve tribes of Israel"; the Jews, obviously, were one of those twelve tribes. "Israel" was another name for Jacob):

> ... Now the sons of Jacob were twelve:
>
> The sons of Leah; Reuben, Jacob's firstborn, and Simeon, and Levi, and Judah, and Issachar, and Zebulun:
>
> The sons of Rachel; Joseph, and Benjamin:
>
> And the sons of Bilhah, Rachel's handmaid; Dan, and Naphtali:
>
> And the sons of Zilpah, Leah's handmaid; Gad, and Asher: these are the sons of Jacob, which were born to him in Padanaram (Genesis 35:22-26)

The Jews were rich owing to their covenant with God, promising them national blessings and inheritance of the Kingdom of God. Lazarus represented Gentiles, outside the rich man's gate, without access to the promises. The parable showed that those who were "in Abraham's bosom"—had the faith of Abraham, and believed and obeyed—would be the ones who would inherit blessings and the Kingdom of God. The beggar was going to take the rich man's place!

Jesus gave a similar parable in Matthew 21:33-49. Here, a man (God) built a vineyard (the promised land, the "land of milk and honey") and rented it out to husbandmen (Israel, including the Jews). But they failed to "render him the fruits in their seasons." They killed the servants and even the son God sent to collect what was due. Jesus warned:

Therefore say I unto you, The kingdom of God shall be taken from you, and given to a nation bringing forth the fruits thereof (Matthew 21:43)

And when the chief priests and Pharisees had heard his parables, they perceived that he spake of them (Matthew 21:45)

The parable of Lazarus and the rich man is not about the afterlife. Jesus staged the parable of Lazarus and the rich man in the common Greek afterlife mythology of that time (torment in hell, etc), knowing His listeners would recognize it as Greek mythology and look for the real meaning.

The parable is about belief and repentance, showing that believing Gentiles would soon be favored over unbelieving Jews. How did the "rich man" fail? He had lacked belief; he failed to obey and repent. He figuratively begged Abraham for help, asking Abraham to send someone from the dead to warn his family. Abraham figuratively replied that they wouldn't believe even if someone rose from the dead.

Perhaps the parable was given about the same time Jesus raised Lazarus, the brother of Martha and Mary, from his tomb. The resurrected Lazarus was being seen daily by all the Jews! Jesus' words about not believing even "though one rose from the dead" (Luke 16:31) would certainly have rung their bells! Or, perhaps, Jesus was referring to His own resurrection, or, to both resurrections.

In Romans chapters 10 and 11 Paul described Israel's (including the Jews) failure due to unbelief, and the opportunity their failure opened for Gentiles. Here are a few passages from Romans:

> But I say, Did not Israel know? First Moses saith, I will provoke you to jealousy by them that are no people, and by a foolish nation I will anger you.
>
> But Esaias is very bold, and saith, I was found of them that sought me not; I was made manifest unto them that asked not after me.
>
> But to Israel he saith, All day long I have stretched forth my hands unto a disobedient and gainsaying people (Romans 10:19-21)
>
> I say then, Have they stumbled that they should fall? God forbid: but rather through their fall salvation is come unto the Gentiles, for to provoke them to jealousy
>
> Now if the fall of them be the riches of the world, and the diminishing of them the riches of the Gentiles; how much more their fulness? (Romans 11:11,12)
>
> Thou wilt say then, The branches [Israel] were broken off, that I [Gentiles] might be graffed in.
>
> Well; because of unbelief they were broken off, and thou standest by faith. Be not highminded, but fear:

> For if God spared not the natural branches, take heed lest he also spare not thee.
>
> Behold therefore the goodness and severity of God: on them which fell, severity; but toward thee, goodness, if thou continue in his goodness: otherwise thou also shalt be cut off (Romans 11:19-22)

Peter describes believers (whether Gentile or of Israel) as *obedient*. By or through faith they have understood the need to obey, and have chosen to do so. Therefore they are in God's mercy—as promised. They are "the people of God" and "an holy nation." The rest are disobedient and remain outside His mercy:

> Unto you therefore which believe he is precious: but unto them which be disobedient, the stone which the builders disallowed, the same is made the head of the corner,
>
> And a stone of stumbling, and a rock of offence, even to them which stumble at the word, being disobedient: whereunto also they were appointed.
>
> But ye are a chosen generation, a royal priesthood, an holy nation, a peculiar people; that ye should shew forth the praises of him who hath called you out of darkness into his marvellous light:
>
> Which in time past were not a people, but are now the people of God: which had not obtained mercy, but now have obtained mercy (1 Peter 2:7-10)

Part Four:

Prophecy for the End of This Age

Wars and rumors of wars. Millions upon millions killed in the World Wars of the 20th century alone, not to mention all the other sad slaughters back through history. Greed, hate, corruption and power struggles, with all the suffering that results: death camps, migrations, refugees, shortages of food, medicine and shelter, lost family members, lost hopes, lost opportunities, wasted talents. It is all unnecessary, and we all know it.

Sure, we have abilities. We have the technology to walk on the moon and explore the universe around us. We can change matter from one form to another. We can explore and manipulate the inner workings of life itself.

No doubt about it: science and technology can—and have—improved the physical quality of our lives. Yet the more technology we have, the closer we come to our own self-destruction. We can destroy each other more quickly and efficiently than ever before. At the push of a button, far-away cities and millions of lives can be destroyed. What we lack is the ability to save ourselves from ourselves.

Regrettably, we will continue on as we have before. We will repeat the sad saga of history.

This book was not written with the intention of explaining Bible prophecy in detail. Perhaps a later book will focus on that. However, a brief overview will help outline the bigger picture of where we are and where we are going.

> **For nation shall rise against nation, and kingdom against kingdom: and there shall be famines, and pestilences, and earthquakes, in divers places.**
>
> **All these are the beginning of sorrows. (Jesus, in Matthew 24:7,8)**
>
> **And this gospel of the kingdom shall be preached in all the world for a witness unto all nations; and then shall the end come. (Matthew 24:14)**

Prophecy shows mankind will come to the brink of self-destruction, a time so bad that "except those days should be shortened," (apparently by divine intervention) we would not survive:

> **For then shall be great tribulation, such as was not since the beginning of the world to this time, no, nor ever shall be.**
>
> **And except those days should be shortened, there should no flesh be saved: but for the elect's sake those days shall be shortened (Matthew 24:21,22)**

So, how will this time of "great tribulation" be shortened?

> **Immediately after the tribulation of those days shall the sun be darkened, and the moon shall not give her light, and the stars shall fall from heaven, and the powers of the heavens shall be shaken:**
>
> **And then shall appear the sign of the Son of man in heaven: and then shall all the tribes of the**

> earth mourn, and they shall see the Son of man coming in the clouds of heaven with power and great glory (Matthew 24:29,30)

Well, there's a game-changer: "lights out." War that would have brought self-destruction comes to a sudden stop as mankind stares in amazement and wonder . . . "What is going on?" And then "the sign of the Son of man" appears in the darkened sky. The whole world will see Jesus "sitting on the right hand of power, and coming in the clouds of heaven" (Matthew 26:64).

> Behold, he cometh with clouds; and every eye shall see him, and they also which pierced him: and all kindreds of the earth shall wail because of him. Even so, Amen. (Revelation 1:7)

> And the glory of the LORD shall be revealed, and all flesh shall see it together: for the mouth of the LORD hath spoken it. (Isaiah 40:5)

> Enter into the rock, and hide thee in the dust, for fear of the LORD, and for the glory of his majesty.

> The lofty looks of man shall be humbled, and the haughtiness of men shall be bowed down, and the LORD alone shall be exalted in that day. (Isaiah 2:10,11)

Suddenly the entire paradigm of our present God-less world evaporates. Seeing is believing. Oh . . . there really IS a God. And Jesus is on the way. Here's the reaction when they see the sign of Jesus coming on His throne:

> And the kings of the earth, and the great men, and the rich men, and the chief captains, and

> the mighty men, and every bondman, and every free man, hid themselves in the dens and in the rocks of the mountains;
>
> And said to the mountains and rocks, Fall on us, and hide us from the face of him that sitteth on the throne, and from the wrath of the Lamb:
>
> For the great day of his wrath is come; and who shall be able to stand? (Revelation 6:15-17)

Sensing this would likely be an appropriate time to get their lives in order, a "great multitude . . . of all nations" come to repentance:

> After this I beheld, and, lo, a great multitude, which no man could number, of all nations, and kindreds, and people, and tongues, stood before the throne, and before the Lamb, clothed with white robes, and palms in their hands (Revelation 7:9)

Having come to repentance, their past sins were "blotted out"; they have figuratively "washed their robes, and made them white in the blood of the Lamb." They are serving God "in his temple"—in His true church—among those in whom He dwells via the holy spirit:

> . . . These are they which came out of great tribulation, and have washed their robes, and made them white in the blood of the Lamb.
>
> Therefore are they before the throne of God, and serve him day and night in his temple: and he that sitteth on the throne shall dwell among them (Revelation 7:14,15)

Part 4: Prophecy for the End of This Age

Prophecy shows that hardships will follow: the world will suffer from what appears to be a nuclear/volcanic winter. Fires rage. A "great mountain, burning with fire" (volcano?) destroys "a third part of the creatures which were in the sea," poisoning "a third part" of fresh waters, and dimming the sun (Revelation chapter 8). More troubles follow, described as "woes" beginning in the ninth chapter of the Revelation.

But Jesus has not yet arrived. Everyone saw Him coming . . . question is: "Where is He?" Jesus warned NOT TO BE DECEIVED because impostors would appear:

Then if any man shall say unto you, Lo, here is Christ, or there; believe it not.

For there shall arise false Christs, and false prophets, and shall shew great signs and wonders; insomuch that, if it were possible, they shall deceive the very elect.

Behold, I have told you before.

Wherefore if they shall say unto you, Behold, he is in the desert; go not forth: behold, he is in the secret chambers; believe it not (Matthew 24:23–26)

What is about to unfold next is described as:

. . . the hour of temptation, which shall come upon all the world, to try them that dwell upon the earth (Revelation 3:10)

For forty-two months a dictatorial "beast" will rule the world, enforcing his/its will and doctrine upon all. With the beast will be a miracle-working "false prophet," perhaps claiming to be an end-time Elijah: he will "bring down fire from heaven in the sight of men," much like the Old Testament prophet Elijah:

> And he doeth great wonders, so that he maketh fire come down from heaven on the earth in the sight of men,
>
> And deceiveth them that dwell on the earth by the means of those miracles which he had power to do in the sight of the beast; saying to them that dwell on the earth, that they should make an image to the beast, which had the wound by a sword, and did live.
>
> And he had power to give life unto the image of the beast, that the image of the beast should both speak, and cause that as many as would not worship the image of the beast should be killed (Revelation 13:13-15)

Together the beast and false prophet will make war against the "saints": the true believers, including those who had only recently come to repentance:

> And it was given unto him to make war with the saints, and to overcome them: and power was given him over all kindreds, and tongues, and nations (Revelation 13:7; Daniel 7:21,25)

Truly this will be "the hour of temptation, which shall come upon all the world, to try them that dwell upon the earth" (Revelation 3:10). The "two witnesses" described in Revelation 11 will be provided beforehand, and will give testimony to the truth for "a thousand two hundred and threescore days" (Revelation 11:3).

> And when they shall have finished their testi-

mony, the beast that ascendeth out of the bottomless pit shall make war against them, and shall overcome them, and kill them.

And their dead bodies shall lie in the street of the great city, which spiritually is called Sodom and Egypt, where also our Lord was crucified (Revelation 11:7,8)

This will be a time of judgment. Every person will have to decide who to believe and follow: the two witnesses, or, the beast and false prophet.

At or near the end of the beast's reign, we have the figurative sounding of the seventh, last trumpet:

And the seventh angel sounded; and there were great voices in heaven, saying, The kingdoms of this world are become the kingdoms of our Lord, and of his Christ; and he shall reign for ever and ever (Revelation 11:15)

This seventh trumpet sounding is that "last trump," when the "dead in Christ" will be resurrected immortal, as we saw in 1 Corinthians 15:50-54 and 1 Thessalonians 4:13-17. Those resurrected—along with those in Christ "which are alive and remain"—will rise "to meet the Lord in the air." Having been born of the spirit—no longer "flesh and blood" (1 Corinthians 15:50)—Jesus will invite them to inherit the Kingdom of God:

Then shall the King say unto them on his right hand, Come, ye blessed of my Father, inherit the kingdom prepared for you from the foundation of the world (Matthew 25:34)

Then God's wrath is poured out on those who remain

on the earth, who worshiped the beast:

> And I heard a great voice out of the temple saying to the seven angels, Go your ways, and pour out the vials of the wrath of God upon the earth.
>
> And the first went, and poured out his vial upon the earth; and there fell a noisome and grievous sore upon the men which had the mark of the beast, and upon them which worshipped his image (Revelation 16:1,2)

During this time the beast and his armies gather at a place called Armageddon, apparently intending to prevent Jesus' arrival at Jerusalem to rule:

> And he gathered them together into a place called in the Hebrew tongue Armageddon (Revelation 6:16)

Jesus returns with His saints, and destroys the beast and its armies:

> And I saw heaven opened, and behold a white horse; and he that sat upon him was called Faithful and True, and in righteousness he doth judge and make war.
>
> His eyes were as a flame of fire, and on his head were many crowns; and he had a name written, that no man knew, but he himself.
>
> And he was clothed with a vesture dipped in blood: and his name is called The Word of God.
>
> And the armies which were in heaven followed him upon white horses, clothed in fine linen,

white and clean (Revelation 19:1-14)

And I saw the beast, and the kings of the earth, and their armies, gathered together to make war against him that sat on the horse, and against his army.

And the beast was taken, and with him the false prophet that wrought miracles before him, with which he deceived them that had received the mark of the beast, and them that worshipped his image. These both were cast alive into a lake of fire burning with brimstone.

And the remnant were slain with the sword of him that sat upon the horse, which sword proceeded out of his mouth: and all the fowls were filled with their flesh (Revelation 19:19-21)

We have already covered the events to follow this. Satan is imprisoned. Jesus rules in full authority, with His saints:

Blessed and holy is he that hath part in the first resurrection: on such the second death hath no power, but they shall be priests of God and of Christ, and shall reign with him a thousand years (Revelation 20:6)

Jesus brings peace:

And it shall come to pass in the last days, that the mountain of the LORD'S house shall be established in the top of the mountains, and shall be exalted above the hills; and all nations shall flow unto it.

> And many people shall go and say, Come ye, and let us go up to the mountain of the LORD, to the house of the God of Jacob; and he will teach us of his ways, and we will walk in his paths: for out of Zion shall go forth the law, and the word of the LORD from Jerusalem.
>
> And he shall judge among the nations, and shall rebuke many people: and they shall beat their swords into plowshares, and their spears into pruninghooks: nation shall not lift up sword against nation, neither shall they learn war any more (Isaiah 2:2-4)

After the thousand years Satan is released, and instigates a rebellion. This will be another time of judgment. Satan and his followers will surround Jerusalem, but they will be destroyed as we saw earlier (Revelation 20:8,9). After this we have the "new heaven and a new earth" where those who received eternal life will live with God forever.

Why?

God is certainly able step in at any time and stop our self-inflicted suffering. But He will not do that until we come to the brink of self-destruction, that time of "great tribulation" Jesus spoke of. And then, as we've seen, Satan will be temporarily removed from the picture. For a thousand years the Kingdom of God—and peace—will rule the world. But then Satan will be released one more (short) time and will poison the peace, seeking to overthrow God's kingdom. Then Satan, and all who follow him, will be destroyed. Only those who received eternal life will remain.

Part 4: Prophecy for the End of This Age

So, why allow evil—and Satan—to continue? Why not just get rid of Satan and put a stop to the suffering? The Bible does not seem to offer a direct, quotable answer. But the pattern and flow of events certainly suggests an answer.

First, the world, under Satanic influence, comes to the point of self-destruction, giving proof that Satan's ways, based on selfish greed, lead to destruction. The proof is "in the pudding."

Then Satan is put out of the way for a time. God's kingdom rules here on earth, bringing peace and plenty for all. Those thousand years prove that God's ways—loving and giving—work. God will be proven right. It will be plain for all to see.

Finally Satan is set free for a short time. His release becomes a time of judgment: those who lived and died during the thousand years—never influenced by Satan—will be tested. Satan leads a final rebellion, inciting to battle:

> **And when the thousand years are expired, Satan shall be loosed out of his prison,**
>
> **And shall go out to deceive the nations which are in the four quarters of the earth, Gog and Magog, to gather them together to battle: the number of whom is as the sand of the sea.**
>
> **And they went up on the breadth of the earth, and compassed the camp of the saints about, and the beloved city: and fire came down from God out of heaven, and devoured them. (Revelation 20:7–9)**

Satan has been proven wrong, twice; he and his followers are finally, and justly, destroyed.

Although God could have destroyed Satan long ago, that would never have proven anything except that God is more powerful. It would never have proven Satan is wrong. Might does not make right; God is a God of justice as well as mercy. So God is providing proof—to all spirit and mortal beings—that He is right and Satan is wrong. God is in control, and is allowing Satan to influence mankind for the time being.

While tempting Jesus, Satan conceded he had been given or allotted power:

> **And the devil, taking him up into an high mountain, shewed unto him all the kingdoms of the world in a moment of time.**
>
> **And the devil said unto him, All this power will I give thee, and the glory of them: for that is delivered unto me; and to whomsoever I will I give it (Luke 4:5,6)**

Satan will be destroyed after being brought down to human mortality:

> **Thine heart was lifted up because of thy beauty, thou hast corrupted thy wisdom by reason of thy brightness: I will cast thee to the ground, I will lay thee before kings, that they may behold thee.**
>
> **Thou hast defiled thy sanctuaries by the multitude of thine iniquities, by the iniquity of thy traffick; therefore will I bring forth a fire from the midst of thee, it shall devour thee, and I will bring thee to ashes upon the earth in the sight of all them that behold thee.**

All they that know thee among the people shall be astonished at thee: thou shalt be a terror, and never shalt thou be any more (Ezekiel 28:17-19)

Mortal life, then, will be the means by which Satan and all his followers will be destroyed. Mortal life is also the means by which God will—and is—creating family. Sons and daughters for the Father's eternal family are being created, right now, through Jesus. They will be given eternal life; they will dwell with Jesus and the Father forever in the new creation—the new heaven and the new earth.

Man was created with free will. It was not a surprise that man would sin and earn death as the wages of sin:

For the wages of sin is death; but the gift of God is eternal life through Jesus Christ our Lord (Romans 6:23)

Redemption from that death penalty was planned right from the beginning. A plan was put in place to make a ransom available to cover our death penalty. The "Word," who was with God "in the beginning . . . was made flesh and dwelt among us" as Jesus (John 1:1-14). His death was planned "from the foundation of the world," to make redemption available for all who would choose to come to repentance, seeking God's ways. Here's Peter, writing to believers:

Forasmuch as ye know that ye were not redeemed with corruptible things, as silver and gold, from your vain conversation received by tradition from your fathers;

But with the precious blood of Christ, as of a lamb

without blemish and without spot:

Who verily was foreordained before the foundation of the world, but was manifest in these last times for you (1 Peter 1:18–20)

The apostle John, while describing those who will worship the beast, mentions that Jesus, the "Lamb," was "slain from the foundation of the world." His death—to make redemption available for us—was planned from the very beginning:

And all that dwell upon the earth shall worship him, whose names are not written in the book of life of the Lamb slain from the foundation of the world (Revelation 13:8)

Just before they left Egypt, Israel was spared from the death angel: the blood of a lamb, sprinkled on their doorways, kept that death angel away. This foreshadowed how God's people would be spared from death through the blood of Jesus, the Lamb of God.

Without the ransom Jesus made available on the cross, we would all be hopelessly doomed to perish in death as the "wages" of our own sin. But now, thanks to Jesus, redemption is possible and available to all. We are promised that mercy, that coverage, that redemption—by grace—if we'll come to God on his terms: in repentance, confessing and forsaking sin.

In repentance, we open our heart and mind to change and spiritual growth, seeking God's will and overcoming slavery to sin. Jesus will work with us through the holy spirit. We'll be made fit, ready, to receive the gift of eternal life as sons and daughters in the Father's family.

Common sense: outside of repentance we will not—can not—change and grow. We will not overcome slavery to sin. We will never be made ready or fit to receive the gift of eternal life. And outside of repentance we receive no mercy. We will perish:

> **. . . except ye repent, ye shall all likewise perish (Jesus, in Luke 13:5)**

> **The Lord is not slack concerning his promise, as some men count slackness; but is longsuffering to us-ward, not willing that any should perish, but that all should come to repentance (2 Peter 3:9)**

Part Five: The Gospel, By Grace

We have all sinned. Our sins have separated us from God (Isaiah 59:1,2) and have earned us "the wages of sin," which is perishing in death, specifically, the second death:

For the wages of sin is death; but the gift of God is eternal life through Jesus Christ our Lord (Romans 6:23)

We need God's mercy. Here's how we can receive His mercy:

He that covereth his sins shall not prosper: but whoso confesseth and forsaketh them shall have mercy (Proverbs 28:13)

Let the wicked forsake his way, and the unrighteous man his thoughts: and let him return unto the LORD, and he will have mercy upon him . . . (Isaiah 55:7)

Mercy is promised if we'll come to repentance: confessing and forsaking sin, turning from a life lived apart from God. Repentance is a state of heart and mind: set on forsaking sin, putting sin out of our life, seeking to do God's will, seeking to please God, no longer living apart from God. If we'll come to repentance our past sins will be blotted out:

Repent therefore and be converted, that your sins may be blotted out, so that times of refreshing may come from the presence of the Lord (Acts 3:19, NKJV; also 2 Peter 1:9 and Romans 3:25)

Our sins were NOT blotted out the moment Jesus died on the cross! Our sins *remain* until we come to repentance!

Part 5: The Gospel, By Grace

Not only will our past sins be forgiven, but the death penalty already earned for those sins will be lifted, covered. We'll be redeemed from that death penalty. Jesus came to serve and "to give His life as a ransom" (Matthew 20:28); He made His death, His blood available to cover the death penalty we earn for sin. That's the work He finished on the cross. Thank you, Jesus.

We can have that mercy, that coverage, that grace, that redemption—as promised—if we'll obey and repent (Acts 17:30) . . . if we'll "come to God" (Hebrews 11:6) on His terms, confessing and forsaking sin (Proverbs 28:13).

If you hear someone preaching "all your sins have been paid for, past, present and future" do not listen to them. Our sins remain—not blotted out—until we come to repentance. We will perish, we will pay for our sins ourselves, unless we come to repentance. Jesus said so:

. . . except ye repent, ye shall all likewise perish (Luke 13:5)

We do not receive saving grace just because we *have* faith. We receive grace *through* faith:

For by grace are ye saved through faith; and that not of yourselves: it is the gift of God (Ephesians 2:8)

Through faith that God exists and rewards, we could and might choose to "come to God" on his terms. Without faith that He exists and rewards we simply *could* not and *would never* choose to come to Him:

But without faith it is impossible to please him: for he that cometh to God must believe that he is, and that he is a rewarder of them that diligently

seek him (Hebrews 11:6)

It is the decision—to obey and "come to God" on His terms—that matters and is pleasing to God . . . and for which we are promised His mercy and grace.

"Faith alone" often paints grace as "unmerited favor." "Unmerited favor" or "easy grace" says we get grace no matter what we do or don't do . . . no merit needed . . . as if we're entitled to it. "Unmerited favor" effectively becomes a license to sin. Yes, there is nothing we can do to *earn* saving grace. If we could somehow *earn* saving grace, there would have been no need for Jesus to die for us. Mercy and redemption by grace are *promised*—not earned—to those who *merit* it by *obeying God's instructions*.

True believing means acting on your faith and obeying. The apostle James used Abraham's example to illustrate that believing goes beyond "faith only." By or through faith Abraham recognized he had a choice to make. He chose to obey; he left for the promised land:

By faith Abraham, when he was called to go out into a place which he should after receive for an inheritance, obeyed; and he went out, not knowing whither he went (Hebrews 11:8)

Later he offered his son Isaac, as he was told to do. For his obedience—"and not by faith only"—Abraham was deemed to be a believer and was justified to God:

But wilt thou know, O vain man, that faith with-without works is dead?

Was not Abraham our father justified by works, when he had offered Isaac his son upon the altar?

> **Seest thou how faith wrought with his works, and by works was faith made perfect?**
>
> **And the scripture was fulfilled which saith, Abraham believed God, and it was imputed unto him for righteousness: and he was called the Friend of God.**
>
> **Ye see then how that by works a man is justified, and not by faith only (James 2:20-24)**

So we see that *believing* goes beyond "faith alone." Faith without works—obedience—is dead. Today Jesus is:

> **. . . the author of eternal salvation unto all them that obey him (Hebrews 5:9)**

Having been "purged" of our "old sins" (2 Peter 1:9) and no longer condemned to perish for past sins, we are no longer separated from God. We enter *justification* or reconciliation with God. We can begin a new life, "times of refreshing" in "the presence of the Lord." How are we in "the presence of the Lord"? Through

> **. . . the Holy Ghost, whom God hath given to them that obey him (Acts 5:32)**

If we will obey and repent, we will receive the holy spirit to help lead us into truth and out of slavery to sin:

> **Then Peter said unto them, Repent, and be baptized every one of you in the name of Jesus Christ for the remission of sins, and ye shall receive the gift of the Holy Ghost (Acts 2:38).**

Jesus' work is not finished. He is at work right now. Jesus says:

> **As many as I love, I rebuke and chasten: be zeal-**

ous therefore, and repent (Jesus, in Revelation 3:19)

Jesus wants us to learn from Him:

Take my yoke upon you, and learn of me; for I am meek and lowly in heart: and ye shall find rest unto your souls (Matthew 11:29)

Through an ongoing relation with Him, abiding in Him (John 15:1-6) through the holy spirit, we are *sanctified*: we become "his workmanship" (Ephesians 2:10); we learn His righteousness. A relationship with Him

. . . yieldeth the peaceable fruit of righteousness unto them which are exercised thereby (Hebrews 12:11)

For we are his workmanship, created in Christ Jesus unto good works, which God hath before ordained that we should walk in them (Ephesians 2:10)

Through the holy spirit, He helps us overcome slavery to sin, preparing us to receive eternal life and to inherit the kingdom of God:

He that overcometh shall inherit all things; and I will be his God, and he shall be my son.

But the fearful, and unbelieving, and the abominable, and murderers, and whoremongers, and sorcerers, and idolaters, and all liars, shall have their part in the lake which burneth with fire and brimstone: which is the second death (Revelation 21:7,8)

But the fruit of the Spirit is love, joy, peace,

longsuffering, gentleness, goodness, faith,

Meekness, temperance: against such there is no law (Galatians 5:22,23)

God wants sons and daughters, to live with Him forever. Creation is not finished: creation of those sons and daughters is in process right now through Jesus:

Wherefore come out from among them, and be ye separate, saith the Lord, and touch not the unclean thing; and I will receive you,

And will be a Father unto you, and ye shall be my sons and daughters, saith the Lord Almighty (2 Corinthians 6:16-18)

Through Him the believer learns to keep God's ten commandments, not just in letter, but in spirit. Twice in Revelation the "saints" are described as those who "keep the commandments of God":

And the dragon was wroth with the woman, and went to make war with the remnant of her seed, which keep the commandments of God, and have the testimony of Jesus Christ. (Revelation 12:17)

Here is the patience of the saints: here are they that keep the commandments of God, and the faith of Jesus. (Revelation 14:12)

While we abide in Him, walking "after the spirit," we remain in justification and are not under condemnation:

There is therefore now no condemnation to them which are in Christ Jesus, who walk not after the flesh, but after the Spirit (Romans 8:1)

While we abide in Him in repentance, He continues, *present tense*, to cover any new sins we commit:

> **But if we walk in the light, as he is in the light, we have fellowship one with another, and the blood of Jesus Christ his Son cleanseth us from all sin (1 John 1:7)**

While we abide in Him, we remain in His grace and have "the hope of salvation." We shall be saved—from ever perishing—when we receive the promised gift of eternal life at Jesus' "revelation," His return:

> **But let us, who are of the day, be sober, putting on the breastplate of faith and love; and for an helmet, the hope of salvation.**
>
> **For God hath not appointed us to wrath, but to obtain salvation by our Lord Jesus Christ (1 Thessalonians 5:8,9; also see Acts 15:11 and Romans 5:9)**
>
> **And this is the promise that he hath promised us, even eternal life (1 John 2:25)**
>
> **Wherefore gird up the loins of your mind, be sober, and hope to the end for the grace that is to be brought unto you at the revelation of Jesus Christ (1 Peter 1:13)**

If we choose to no longer abide in Him in repentance, no longer walking "after the spirit," we return to condemnation. We are no longer in His "goodness" or grace and will be "cut off," forfeiting our hope of salvation:

> **If a man abide not in me, he is cast forth as a branch, and is withered; and men gather them,**

> and cast them into the fire, and they are burned (Jesus, in John 15:6)
>
> For if God spared not the natural branches [the Israelites], take heed lest he also spare not thee.
>
> Behold therefore the goodness and severity of God: on them which fell, severity; but toward thee, goodness, if thou continue in his goodness: otherwise thou also shalt be cut off (Romans 11:21,22)
>
> Let us therefore fear, lest, a promise being left us of entering into his rest, any of you should seem to come short of it (Hebrews 4:1)

Outside of repentance, we receive no mercy. We will surely perish in death, without redemption from the death penalty we've earned for sin. That's why Jesus warned,

> . . . except ye repent, ye shall all likewise perish (Luke 13:5)

That's why Jesus told His disciples to preach "repentance and remission of sins" . . . not "faith alone" and not "just trust Jesus" as so many today are preaching:

> Then opened he their understanding, that they might understand the scriptures,
>
> And said unto them, Thus it is written, and thus it behoved Christ to suffer, and to rise from the dead the third day:
>
> And that repentance and remission of sins should be preached in his name among all nations, beginning at Jerusalem (Luke 24:45-47)

What did John the Baptist preach?

. . . the word of God came unto John the son of Zacharias in the wilderness.

And he came into all the country about Jordan, preaching the baptism of repentance for the remission of sins (Luke 3:3,4)

Come to repentance, and you're promised remission of past sins. Come to repentance, and a new life, "times of refreshing," can begin "in the presence of the Lord": through the gift of the holy spirit. Outside of repentance—that heart and mind willing to change—He can not work with us.

The apostle Peter wrote that God does not want anyone to perish. God wants all men to come to repentance:

The Lord is not slack concerning his promise, as some men count slackness; but is longsuffering to us-ward, not willing that any should perish, but that all should come to repentance (2 Peter 3:9)

In the following passage Paul touches on: grace, repentance, redemption, sanctification and the hope of salvation at Jesus' return. Jesus died for us, so that He "might"—would be able to—redeem us from the death penalty we've earned for sin. He made His own death available for us, available to cover our death penalty:

For the grace of God that bringeth salvation hath appeared to all men,

Teaching us that, denying ungodliness and worldly lusts, we should live soberly, righteously, and godly, in this present world;

Looking for that blessed hope, and the glorious

appearing of the great God and our Saviour Jesus Christ;

Who gave himself for us, that he might redeem us from all iniquity, and purify unto himself a peculiar people, zealous of good works (Titus 2:11–14)

Did you notice that Paul made no mention of "faith alone"? Faith alone is not enough: true believers are those who—like Abraham—act on their faith and obey God. They "come to God" on His terms. For that they receive His promised mercy and enter into "his goodness": His grace. In His grace, by His grace, they will see salvation.

If you hear someone preaching "faith alone" or "just trust" do not listen to them. They are preaching a lie. "Faith alone" or "faith + nothing = salvation" says nothing other than faith is required. Please recognize "faith alone" for what it really is: a sneaky, underhanded way of saying neither repentance nor obedience are necessary! That has been great news for itching ears ever since Martin Luther came up with it hundreds of years ago.

In Ephesians 1:12,13 Paul illustrates and brings to life the sequence of events that brought the Ephesians to receipt of the holy spirit. First, they heard the gospel of salvation and they trusted: they had faith. They also believed: they committed, they took action and obeyed the gospel. They "stepped off their boat." For *that*, they received the gift of the holy spirit:

That we should be to the praise of his glory, who first trusted in Christ.

In whom ye also trusted, after that ye heard

> **the word of truth, the gospel of your salvation: in whom also after that ye believed, ye were sealed with that holy Spirit of promise (Ephesians 1:12,13)**

After they believed—committed and obeyed—they received the holy spirit. Now we can learn something by connecting some dots: we can confirm that true believing goes beyond faith or trust, and includes obedience. Who is it that receives the holy spirit? Scripture confirms: it's those who obey . . . not those who just have faith or trust:

> **And we are his witnesses of these things; and so is also the Holy Ghost, whom God hath given to them that obey him (Acts 5:32)**

And what does God tell us to do?

> **And the times of this ignorance God winked at; but now commandeth all men every where to repent (Acts 17:30)**

And what do we receive when we obey and come to repentance? The holy spirit:

> **Then Peter said unto them, Repent, and be baptized every one of you in the name of Jesus Christ for the remission of sins, and ye shall receive the gift of the Holy Ghost (Acts 2:38)**

So we see that "faith alone" is not enough to receive the holy spirit. We must be true believers, acting on our faith by obeying and coming to God in repentance. Then we'll receive the holy spirit. True believing goes beyond "faith alone" or "just trust" or "faith + nothing"!

Acts 3:19 confirms this. We enter "the presence of the

Lord" (via the holy spirit) after coming to repentance:

> **Repent therefore and be converted, that your sins may be blotted out, so that times of refreshing may come from the presence of the Lord (Acts 3:19, NKJV)**

Through the holy spirit Jesus and the Father will dwell in us. They will make their "abode" in us:

> **Jesus answered and said unto him, If a man love me, he will keep my words: and my Father will love him, and we will come unto him, and make our abode with him. (John 14:23)**

To have Jesus and the Father dwell in us and love us . . . *this* is the water of life. ***This is life as it was designed to be.*** Outside of knowing them, we have a spiritual thirst that cannot be quenched. Knowing them and abiding in them, is a "well of water springing up into everlasting life":

> **But whosoever drinketh of the water that I shall give him shall never thirst; but the water that I shall give him shall be in him a well of water springing up into everlasting life (John 4:14)**

God knows we are sinners. He stands ready to help us with that. But that is only possible if we are in repentance, having a heart and mind willing and commited to change.

Jesus says:

> **Behold, I stand at the door, and knock: if any man hear my voice, and open the door, I will come in to him, and will sup with him, and he with me (Revelation 3:20)**